No one that I know is better equipped, better qualified, and has the spiritual credentials and credibility to expound the issues in Hindu-Christian dialogue with the integrity and honesty it calls for. For Rambachan, engaging in interfaith relations and dialogue is not only an academic and relational issue, but also—perhaps more so—a spiritual exercise. It is not surprising that the first comprehensive and compelling volume on Hindu-Cristian dialogue comes from him.

—S. Wesley Ariarajah, professor emeritus of ecumenical theology, Drew University School of Theology, Madison, NJ; former director of the Interfaith Dialogue program of the World Council of Churches

Praise for *Pathways to Hindu-Christian Dialogue*

Pathways to Hindu-Christian Dialogue is the fruit of Anantanand Rambachan's lifetime of reflection and conversation, deep theological learning, and patient commitment to dialogue as understood and practiced at home and abroad. He shows us in a simple and direct way, free of jargon and from the heart, the ever-greater value of dialogue in today's fractured and intolerant world. Hindus and Christians, and believers in every tradition, will want to travel the wise and serene pathway Rambachan clears for us.

> —Francis X. Clooney, SJ, Parkman Professor of Divinity, Harvard University, and first president of the Society for Hindu-Christian Studies

Pathways to Hindu-Christian Dialogue is a thoughtful and thought-provoking series of essays on the blessings, challenges, and possibilities inherent in Hindu-Christian dialogue. Based on his own decades-long experience in the field, Prof. Rambachan presents his reflections with the intellectual rigor of a scholar and the humility of an earnest seeker of truth.

> —Swami Tyagananda, head of the Ramakrishna Vedanta Society, Boston, and Hindu chaplain, Harvard University and MIT

Anantanand Rambachan offers a superb reflection on Hindu-Christian dialogue based on decades of his own committed participation. He wonderfully integrates personal narrative and theological analysis as an accomplished scholar and Hindu practitioner who is deeply acquainted with Christian life and thought. He clarifies the reasons for dialogue as the shared quest for meaning, friendship, and the moral imperative to work together to transform structures of injustice in a shared affirmation of human dignity. He also provides unsparing critique of both Christian and Hindu triumphalism and of caste, as well as profound insights into the core vision and concepts of each tradition. This book will be essential reading for anyone interested in interfaith dialogue and is a worthy complement to Rambachan's landmark work, *A Hindu Theology of Liberation*.

—Kusumita P. Pedersen, professor emerita of religious studies, St. Francis College, Brooklyn Heights, NY

In Dr. Anantanand Rambachan, who lives his life according to the Hindu religious tradition, I see a marvelous example of Hindu initiative to dialogue with Christians. Dr. Rambachan is aware of the significant evolution that the Hindu religious tradition has been undergoing. Though fundamentally different one from the other, Hindu and Christian religious traditions have much in common to engage in a fruitful dialogue for the benefit of both and especially for the common good of society, where these traditions are lived, especially in India. Dr. Rambachan challenges Christians to have an appreciation of Hinduism in order to overcome the present state of unease. Going beyond the general tendency to dwell on apparent analogies with facile irenicism, and avoiding superficial compromise, Dr. Anantanand Rambachan encourages friendship on a deeper level between Hindus and Christians, whose traditions, though different, could become occasions for mutual enrichment and engagement in creative dialogue for a peaceful and harmonious society. The book *Pathways to Hindu-Christian Dialogue* brings out emphatically an encouraging message for a fruitful Hindu-Christian dialogue.

—Archbishop Felix Machado, Secretary General of the Catholic Bishops' Conference of India, Vasai, India

Pathways to
Hindu-Christian
Dialogue

Pathways to Hindu-Christian Dialogue

Anantanand Rambachan

Fortress Press

Minneapolis

PATHWAYS TO HINDU-CHRISTIAN DIALOGUE

Cover image: Tim Mossholder on Unsplash.com
Cover design: Savanah N. Landerholm

Print ISBN: 978-1-5064-7460-1
eBook ISBN: 978-1-5064-7461-8

For my Christian friends in dialogue

Contents

Foreword

Of all the dialogical relationships that Christians have cultivated with the other major religious traditions of the world, Hindu-Christian relations are perhaps the least developed. This is not because there has not been sufficient contact and relationship between the two traditions. Historically, there have been a number of thriving Syrian Christian communities in the southwestern parts of India from at least the second century CE, and an oral tradition maintains that the apostle Thomas himself brought the gospel to India in 52 CE. Although this specific claim has not been historically verified, there is no doubt that the Christian presence in India and its encounter with Hinduism go back to the early centuries of Christian history. It is of interest that this early encounter was, in fact, so cordial and dialogical that Saint Thomas Christians were considered Christian in religion, Hindu in culture, and Oriental in worship.[1]

However, the major encounter between Christianity and Hinduism took place during the eighteenth- and nineteenth-century Christian missionary outreach into many parts of the world, including the Indian subcontinent. This missionary outreach took place in the context of the colonization of much of Asia by Western powers, and this historical reality played a major role in shaping Hindu-Christian relations for much of the rest of history. Colonization primarily had to do with trade but was accompanied by a conviction on the part of the colonizers that their cultures, religions, and ways of life were far superior to that of those being colonized. Christianity, which had aligned itself with empires since the time of the Roman emperor Constantine, had incorporated much of this sense of superiority into its self-understanding. One of the significant differences between the colonization of Latin America and Asia, however, is that the colonial powers did not forcefully introduce Christianity into the regions but provided the context in which the missionary movement could promote Christianity.

There had not been a uniform response to Hinduism on the part of individual missionaries; one can trace wide-ranging approaches, from the total rejection of Hinduism as superstition to a deep appreciation of its spiritual heritage. But perhaps the most appropriate word that would describe the initial response of Christians to Hinduism is *bewilderment.* Christianity is a founded religion with a single founder, with one scriptural canon widely accepted by the community and with its basic teachings codified into creeds, doctrines, and dogmas. It also developed a magisterium or a centralized teaching authority that sought to preserve the purity of the doctrines. In many ways, it was everything that Hinduism was not. As a traditional religion with no specific founder, incorporating almost all the spiritual streams that arose within India for over three thousand years, with a multiplicity of ways the ultimate reality is conceived and responded to and many ways of practicing the faith, Hinduism presented a daunting challenge to Christianity. Questions like "Who is a Hindu?" "What is Hinduism?" and "Who or which community represented the traditions?" were as ambiguous then as they are to this day. There is a real sense that Christians were not sure how to identify the Hindu partner for dialogue. Christians also found the highly stratified social organization based on levels of ritual purity and the plight of women in society difficult to deal with.

From the Hindu perspective, Christianity presented itself as an intolerant and arrogant religion. Hindus could not understand why God, whom both religious traditions acknowledge as the Creator of the universe, would reveal Godself only in the history of Israel and in the life, death, and resurrection of Jesus of Nazareth. The Christian claim of being in possession of the "whole truth" and the "only way" for salvation or liberation also presented an unsurmountable problem to the Hindus. Even more troubling was the Christian attitude to religious plurality, which discounted the validity of other religious traditions and expected everyone to become part of the Christian community.

Perhaps the most troubling to the Hindus was the Christian understanding of mission. Hinduism believed in the right of persons who have had any form of spiritual enlightenment to share it with others, as the Lord Buddha, Mahavira, and Guru Nanak did, and to bring their followers into a believing community. Although there had been confrontations among these traditions, including brief periods of persecution, gradually, the traditions settled down into kind of sister religious traditions. But Christianity was unable to accept religious plurality and, at least in theory, sought to replace the religious traditions of India with Christianity. The rhetoric of "bringing India to Christ" persists to this day among Christian conservative circles. Conversion and the Christian intention to create a culturally and religiously alternate community continues to bedevil Hindu-Christian relations. Although Christianity in India has undergone many changes and some of the colonial dimensions of Christianity have been shed by most Indian mainline churches in our day, the Hindu image of Christianity as an intolerant religion continues to persist.

This does not mean that there have not been more beneficial relationships as a result of the arrival of Christianity in India. Christianity introduced modern education and health care into India and provided the inspiration for a number of social reform movements within India. Many who found the missionary movement and the church to be a problem still took inspiration from the life and teachings of Jesus. However, today, the rise of the Hindu nationalist movement, Hindutva, challenging the legitimacy of Christianity and Islam as part of the Indian religious life has brought new challenges to this relationship.

These realities make an exploration of Hindu-Christian dialogue a challenging and arduous task. One needs to have an informed understanding of both Christianity and Hinduism as well as a firm grasp of the principles, dimensions, and goals of interfaith dialogue to be able to discuss it. One should also be able to affirm what is positive in other religions and state clearly where one disagrees with them. More importantly, one should have the humility to be able to be self-critical about one's own tradition.

Anantanand Rambachan has deep knowledge of both traditions, has developed friendships across the two traditions from his school days, and has had many decades of sustained involvement in Hindu-Christian and multilateral dialogues organized by the World Council of Churches, the Pontifical Council for Interreligious Dialogue, and international interfaith organizations like Religions for Peace, Parliament of the World's Religions, and so on. I have personal knowledge of the history of his involvement in interfaith dialogue as a practicing Hindu, equaled by his excellent academic credentials.

No one that I know is better equipped or better qualified and has the spiritual credentials and credibility to expound the issues in Hindu-Christian dialogue with the integrity and honesty it calls for. For Rambachan, interfaith relations and dialogue is not only an academic and relational issue but also, perhaps more so, a spiritual exercise. It is not surprising that the first, most comprehensive and compelling volume on Hindu-Christian dialogue comes from him.

S. Wesley Ariarajah
August 2021

Introduction

I was born in the twin-island nation of Trinidad and Tobago, the southernmost in the chain of Caribbean islands stretching from the Gulf of Mexico to the South American mainland. Trinidad sits 6.8 miles off the coast of Venezuela.

I am a descendant of Indians, primarily Hindus and Muslims, who were brought to Trinidad starting in 1845 to replace emancipated Africans who refused to continue working on sugar plantations and who chose instead to become small independent farmers. Harsh measures to induce them back to the land included laws against squatting and heavy taxes on land and buildings not connected with sugar cultivation. These efforts, however, proved futile. The survival of the plantation economy was threatened, and Chinese and Portuguese workers, recruited to replace Africans, drifted into business or private agriculture as soon as their contracts expired. India proved to be the most suitable source of individuals with the required labor skills and provided a steady stream of immigrants from 1845 when the first group of laborers arrived in Trinidad until 1917 when the system was abolished.

Indian immigrants to the West Indies came under a system of indentureship. The labor contracts were generally for a period of five years in the case of males and three years for females. At the end of this period, immigrants could reindenture themselves, return to India, or receive a gift of state land. Seventy-one percent of the indentured workers chose to make their homes in Trinidad. The reasons for emigration were many. In several instances, force was employed, and misleading information was provided by recruiting agents. Some migrated out of a love for adventure, while others were fleeing the hands of British law for their involvement in the 1857 uprising against the British. In the main, however, emigrants were seeking escape from the effects of frequent famines in the provinces of northern India. The main port of embarkation was Kolkata (Chennai and Mumbai were occasionally used), and the majority of Indians came from the northern districts of the United Provinces and Bihar.

The population of Trinidad and Tobago is approximately 1.4 million, with an area of 1,850 square miles, and it is home to astonishing religious, cultural, and ethnic diversity. The major religions are Christianity, Hinduism, and Islam, but there are also practitioners of African traditions that include Shango and Orisha as well as syncretic communities, like the Spiritual Baptists, integrating Christian and African traditions. All of these traditions were vitally present in my small southern village, with mosques, churches, Hindu temples, and home shrines. I had friends from all of these communities. We understood the significance of the echoing evening drumming from the African shrines and knew the religious calendars observed by our Muslim and Christian neighbors. In times of illness, we sought the help of a revered Muslim elder in our village who was knowledgeable about traditional Indian medicines and therapies.

I was born in a Hindu family, and religious diversity was a natural part of my childhood. I never thought it should be otherwise. We welcomed Christian choirs who went from home to home singing carols on the evenings before Christmas, and we received special treats from our Muslim neighbors when they celebrated Eid ul Fitr to mark the end of fasting during the month of Ramadan. We shared traditional meals with our neighbors of other faiths on the occasion of the Hindu festival of Diwali. I admired the discipline and commitment of my Muslim high school friends who observed the fast. For my high school education, I attended a very diverse school founded by Canadian Christian Presbyterian missionaries. School mornings started with Christian worship that offered opportunities for learning more about that tradition.

Learning about other traditions came as a natural consequence of growing up in a diverse community and from childhood friendships. Such learning took a formal turn when I was in graduate school at the University of Leeds in the United Kingdom, where I took courses on Christian history and theology with the late Professor David Jenkins, who later became bishop of Durham, and courses on Islam and Islamic mysticism with Professor Bill Weaver. My learning about the Christian tradition continued with my appointment to teach in the Religion Department at Saint Olaf College in Northfield, Minnesota, in the United States, a four-year liberal arts institution of higher education affiliated with the Lutheran Christian tradition. I had the opportunity to team-teach comparative theology courses with and learn from several of my Christian colleagues.[1]

My deepest learning about the Christian tradition, however, has come through dialogue with Christian theologians and practitioners over the past four decades. In this book, I describe some of the conversations and meetings in which I participated, starting in 1981 when I was invited by the World Council of Churches to attend a Hindu-Christian dialogue meeting on "Religious Resources for a Just Society" in the small North Indian, Himalayan town of Rajpur. My involvement in the dialogue program of the World Council of Churches has continued to this day, and I have had the privilege of participating in general assemblies in Vancouver, Canada; Canberra, Australia; Harare, Zimbabwe; and Porto Alegre, Brazil. I also had the honor of addressing the assemblies in Harare and Porto Alegre. During these decades, I had the privilege of working with dialogue leaders at the World Council of Churches, including Stanley J. Samartha, John B. Taylor, S. Wesley Ariarajah, Hans Ucko, Shanta D. Premawardhana, and most recently, Peniel J. R. Rajkumar.

I have also had a long relationship with the Vatican's Pontifical Council for Interreligious Dialogue, through which I had the honor of meeting Pope John Paul II, Pope Benedict, and Pope Francis. Most recently, over the two-year period of 2016–18, I participated in a series of "Ethics in Action" consultations at Casina Pio IV in the Vatican Gardens. Convened as a partnership among the Pontifical Academy for Social Sciences, the United Nations Sustainable Development Solutions Network, the University of Notre Dame, and Religions for Peace, these meetings brought together leaders and scholars from religious and scientific backgrounds, businesses, and private foundations to consider the moral dimensions of sustainable development. The topics included poverty, peace, migration, corporate responsibility, education, the environment, Indigenous peoples, corruption, and employment.[2]

These meetings, and others too numerous to mention, were great sources of my learning about Christian and other traditions, as well as about my own. I was constantly challenged to think critically about the Hindu tradition and to creatively and authentically retrieve resources for addressing diverse contemporary issues. On topics such as migration, corruption, and corporate responsibility, there was little or no systematic Hindu reflection. Learning from the resources and methodology of other traditions helped me discern and apply relevant teachings within the Hindu tradition. For the enrichment of these dialogues, I am immensely grateful.

Among the greatest gifts that I continue to receive from dialogue is friendship. Some of my deepest and longest-lasting friendships were formed through interreligious dialogue. It is especially difficult to identify the impact and significance of these relationships, some of which have lasted for more than four decades. I encounter the Christian tradition in a very special way through its embodiment in friends who express that faith in their way of life. For these friendships, I remain grateful and recollect the words of Rabindranath Tagore, India's Nobel Prize–winning poet, speaking of friendship: "Thou hast made me known to friends whom I knew not. Thou hast given me seats in homes not my own. Thou hast brought the distant near and made a brother of the stranger. I am uneasy at heart when I have to leave my accustomed shelter; I forgot that there abides the old in the new, and that there also thou abides."[3]

This book is one of the fruits of these friendships, and I hope that my Christian friends will recognize our journey together, our shared experiences, and their impact on me through these words. Their names are too numerous to mention them all. Among these are S. Wesley Ariarajah, Hans Ucko, M. Thomas Thangaraj, Heidi Hadsell, Harold Coward, Catherine Cornille, Archbishop Felix Machado, Bishop Clyde Harvey, Luzia Wehrle, Peniel Rajkumar, Sathianathan Clarke, Jay T. Rock, Shanta Premawardhana, Diana Eck, John Thatamanil, William Vendley, Francis Clooney, and Bradley Malkovsky. My religious life has been and continues to be enriched by these relationships. I have benefited immeasurably from the opportunity to converse and interact with these friends, and I know that my spiritual poverty would be much greater without the wealth I continue to receive from them.

This is not a book of theories about Hindu-Christian dialogue. It is a book about the practice and experience of dialogue, and I write as a practitioner who is deeply influenced by engagement in dialogue. I imagine my primary readers to be Hindus and Christians who live in diverse communities, who wish to build relationships, learn with and from each other, and work together for justice and human dignity.

I do not write with naivety and innocence about the ongoing tensions and conflicts between Hindus and Christians;

I am painfully aware of these as I write. I also do not overlook or minimize the theological differences between Hindus and Christians. Ignoring or trivializing such distinctions does not foster truth and integrity in relationships and dialogue. We participate in dialogue not to dissolve differences but to understand them and build relationships of trust that enable us to work together for the common good.

I continue to engage in dialogue because, in spite of the lingering scars of the past and the conflicts of the present, in spite of our different theological claims, I believe that animosity and mistrust ought not to circumscribe the relationships that are possible for Hindus and Christians. We have much to learn from each other. There is an ongoing need to build relationships that are nurtured in the soil of mutual understanding, trust, and love. Dialogue is a journey of hope, but we have no alternative way of journeying in communities of diversity. Those of us who have traveled together in friendship have reasons for hope. We have experienced the joys of crossing boundaries, overcoming estrangement, finding common ground, and discovering our common humanity. We know that we are incomplete without each other.

My most fundamental reason for welcoming and engaging in Hindu-Christian dialogue, as I have described in various places in this book, is theological. Following the description of God in the Taittirīya Upaniṣad (3.1.1; "That from which all beings originate, by which they are sustained and to which they return"), I believe God to be the origin, source, and destiny of every being. God is not an ethnic, tribal, or national deity. The Bhagavadgītā (9.17) speaks of God as father and mother of the entire universe.[4] As a Hindu, my understanding of God makes it contradictory to propose that God is anything but one or that human beings do not belong to a single community. Upaniṣad accounts of creation always begin with the singular existence of God as the source of all that exists.[5] In the words of the Chāndogya Upaniṣad (6.2.1), "In the beginning, dear one, this was Being alone, one only, without a second."[6] At the same time, the Ṛg Veda (1.164.46; "The One Being, the wise speak of in many ways") affirms that we speak in different, even contradictory, ways about this one. As a Hindu, I affirm the reality of multiple understandings while denying multiple divinities. Hindu teachings enable me to think of persons in other traditions not as strangers with alien, false, or rival deities but as fellow beings whose God is our God. At the eighth assembly of the World Council of Churches in Zimbabwe (1998), I spoke of God as not yours or mine but ours. God does not belong to us; we belong to God. Our acknowledgment of God, I said, ought to be the starting point for seeking engagement and relationship with one another and for building the bonds of trust that will enable us to question and learn from one another. In this way, we may all hope to grow in our understanding of God, our God. This is not an uncritical dismissal of differences as semantic but a profound acknowledgment of the reality of difference with admitting the unity and oneness of the divine. One of the purposes of dialogue is the continuing pursuit of understanding the theological meaning of our differences.

Thinking of friends of other traditions as being oriented toward the same divine being fills me with the joyous excitement of recognizing a new relationship. It enlarges my understanding of the boundaries of religious community that now includes all who understand themselves in relation to this one. It motivates me to build dialogical relationships with those whose lives are centered on this one. I am eager to learn what my friends know of this one being about whom my tradition also speaks. I want to share my knowledge of the One and be enriched by their experiences. Dialogue excites me.

There is another important and complementary theological justification, from the Hindu tradition, for my commitment to dialogue. Although the different ways in which we understand

and speak of God are important, it is a core Hindu teaching that our words and symbols are inadequate and that the ultimate is always more than we could define, describe, or understand with our finite minds. A God whose nature and essence could be fully captured in our words or who could be contained within the boundaries of the human mind would not be the absolute taught in Hinduism. A famous verse from the Taittirīya Upaniṣad (2.4) speaks of the absolute as "that from which all words, along with the mind, turn back, having failed to grasp." Other texts caution us that the infinite is not to be comprehended or thought of in the same manner that we think of finite objects in the world. The Kena Upaniṣad (chap. 2), speaking of the absolute, reminds us that our words do not go there; speech fails, but the act of speaking is made possible only by the presence of the divine.

The Hindu acknowledgment of the limits of our language and understanding is a justification for professing our traditions and engaging others with humility. If we admit the limits of our theologies, we must be ready to learn from and be enriched by what other traditions teach about the nature of God. I acknowledge in this work that my own religious life as a Hindu has been and continues to be enriched by my encounters with practitioners of other traditions. I think of myself as a fellow traveler on a vast highway who has discovered that he is surrounded by other travelers with stories full of wisdom, profound experiences, and unanticipated discoveries. I have benefited immeasurably from the opportunity to converse and interact with some of these pilgrims. For this I am grateful, and this book is one of the expressions of my indebtedness and gratitude.

This book is divided into seven chapters. Chapter 1 ("Starting Points for Hindu-Christian Dialogue") uses as its opening point a meeting on conversion in Lariano, Italy (2006). This meeting culminated, some years later, in the publication titled

"Christian Witness in a Multi-religious World: Recommendations for Conduct." Although the Hindu tradition welcomes the sharing of religious teaching, Hindus become uneasy and suspicious of grand plans, programs, and resources aimed at conversion and of the development of missionary strategies targeting particular religious communities. In this context, the preamble to "Christian Witness in a Multi-religious World," which speaks of the centrality of mission for Christians, is not helpful for engagement with Hindus. In this chapter, I suggest alternative starting points. These include the unity of the divine as the source of all life, the limits of human understanding, the unity of the human community, learning from one another in mutual respect and humility, and addressing together the causes of human suffering.

Chapter 2 ("Theological Resources and Challenges to Hindu-Christian Dialogue") discusses Hindu-Christian dialogue through a number of important questions. These include, Are Hindus interested in dialogue with Christians? Is dialogue a Christian problem? Is there anything to discuss? Are there no differences? Is there anything to learn? Is there a future for Hindu-Christian dialogue? Through these questions, I identify some of the challenges for Hindu-Christian dialogue, as well as reasons for my hope.

Chapter 3 ("Hindu Nationalism [Hindutva] and Hindu-Christian Dialogue") discusses the ideology of Hindutva (Hinduness) and its implications for Hindu-Christian dialogue. For V. S. Savarkar, Christians are alien communities in India, since they do not satisfy his definition of Hinduness. Meaningful dialogue between Hindus and Christians is not possible as long as Christians are excluded in this way and their national commitments are questioned. Dialogue requires the affirmation of the religious identity of our partners. Hindutva champions a form of majority rule that appears to be intolerant of plural identities by asserting a definition of nationality and loyalty that excludes large numbers of people for whom India is home. Such definitions also raise crucial questions about religion and the status of the nation, the nature of Hinduism as a world religion, and Hinduism's role in world affairs. Hindus must lift their voices in concern against ideologies that are intolerant of plural religious identities or make demands that violate personal integrity and religious freedom.

Chapter 4 ("Caste and Hindu-Christian Dialogue") begins with the acknowledgment that the majority of Christians in India are Dalits. It should be obvious that people from the untouchable castes experience the Hindu tradition as oppressive and as negating their dignity and self-worth. In place of earnest efforts to understand this fact, Hindus treat the converts as ignorant and simple-minded, subject to easy manipulation and deceit. Conversion is a challenge but also an opportunity for Hindu leaders to consider the relationship between religious doctrine and practice and systemic social and economic structures that condemn millions to lives of poverty, indignity, and exclusion from full participation in the tradition. The tradition needs to go beyond regarding the convert as a childlike individual who needs to always be protected from the lures and deceptive practices of missionaries. At the same time, the persistence of caste in other communities, even after conversion, points to it having a transreligious nature. This must be recognized and affirmed by both traditions and become the basis of mutual support and cooperation for the overcoming of oppressive systems of human hierarchy and the promotion of human flourishing.

Chapter 5 ("What Can Hindus Learn from Christianity?") begins with identifying a few significant Hindu teachers and leaders who acknowledge learning from Christianity. I also offer a more personal account of learning from the Christian tradition. Dialogue with Christian partners and friends who are also grappling with racism and other structures of systemic injustice in Christian communities has helped me become aware of such structures within my own tradition and hear the voices of the marginalized who experience my tradition as oppressive. On the constructive side, they also help me discern the theological resources within the Hindu tradition that I could retrieve to show why we cannot be indifferent to injustice and why we must argue for relationships that affirm the equal dignity of every human being and that exemplify compassion and justice. I reflect also on what Hindus may learn from a suffering and crucified God.

In chapter 6 ("What Can Christians Learn from Hinduism?"), I identify some significant insights from the Hindu tradition that may open doors to deeper dialogue, learning, and mutual enrichment. These include Hindu understandings of the God-universe relationship, the human problem, and the nature of liberation. Both the Hindu and Christian traditions propose a fundamental problem to be overcome but describe these differently. For the Christian tradition, the emphasis is on original sin; Hindus speak of ignorance (*avidyā*). Because of sin, we live in a fallen state from which we need help to be saved. The consequences of sin and ignorance, however, are quite similar: egocentrism, greed, separation, and alienation. How could thinking about the human problem as one of original ignorance complement or enrich Christian thinking about original sin? In a similar way, the Hindu emphasis on liberation here and now, in this world, could be a meaningful place for Hindu-Christian learning and dialogue.

Chapter 7 ("The Political and the Theological: Why Hindu-Christian Dialogue?") explores what I regard as the two most important justifications for Hindu-Christian dialogue: the political and the theological. Hindus and Christians can stand on common ground in affirming human dignity and worth that spring from the divine presence in the human. This living out of this truth requires work to overcome structures of inequality, indignity, and injustice. For both of our traditions, the life of generosity and compassion expresses best the meaning of liberation. Political arguments for dialogue, though necessary, are not sufficient. What distinguishes interreligious dialogue from other types of conversations is the fact that we are engaging one another from the depths of our religious commitments. Surely, the nature of these commitments must inform the fundamental reasons why we reach out to our neighbors of other faiths. Questions such as the following cannot be ignored: What, for us, is the theological significance of people of other faiths? Do we have a theological need for them? Why is our world better because of religious diversity? Answers to such questions are important if the justification for dialogue must transcend the political. Such answers must emerge uniquely from each tradition, and dialogue would enable traditions to develop such responses. I offer personal answers to such questions.

It is my hope that this work would contribute to building and deepening relationships and understanding among Hindus and Christians in different parts of our world. May the reverence for one another's humanity that is at the heart of our traditions inspire us to share and receive in dialogue. The highest teachings of our traditions do not turn us away from our neighbors in need or deafen us to their cries. Our understanding of God is not true unless it finds active expression in lives of loving compassion and in work that aims to alleviate suffering. May our dialogue find fulfillment in the humble privilege of serving God in all beings.

I want to express my gratitude to Professor S. Wesley Ariarajah, a distinguished pioneer and leader of interreligious dialogue in our times, for contributing a foreword to my book. I am grateful to my editor at Fortress Press, Dr. Jesudas Athyal, for his confidence in me and his enthusiasm for this book. My wife, Geeta, is an abiding source of support, encouragement, and faith. She diligently reads and offers critiques on all of my writings. I am forever grateful to her.

CHAPTER ONE

Starting Points for Hindu-Christian Dialogue

In 2006, I was a participant in a consultation in Lariano, Italy (May 12–16), convened by the Pontifical Council for Interreligious Dialogue and the Office of Interreligious Relations and Dialogue of the World Council of Churches. The conference was titled "Conversion-Assessing the Reality," and with participants of different traditions (Buddhist, Christian, Islamic, Jewish, Yoruban), we offered our reflections on the matter of conversion.[1] A second meeting, an intra-Christian consultation, was held in Toulouse, France (2007), and a final intra-Christian meeting took place in Bangkok, Thailand (2011). This is the meeting that finalized the document "Christian Witness in a Multi-religious World: Recommendations for Conduct" (CWMW).[2] I am delighted to note that several of our recommendations from Lariano appeared in the final document.

At Lariano, we affirmed the right to freedom of religion, which includes the freedom to practice one's own faith, to share one's faith with people of one's own and other faiths, and to embrace another faith. At the same time, we noted that the sharing of faiths must be done in ways that do not violate the rights and religious sensibilities of others. We asked that conversion by unethical means be rejected and for transparency in the practice of inviting others to one's faith. We invited traditions to move away from the exclusive focus on converting others. We called upon faiths to reject and discourage unethical methods of conversion that include taking advantage of human beings in vulnerable situations and offering humanitarian aid as incentives for conversion. We concluded our report with a call for continuing interreligious dialogue on conversion.

The matter of mission and conversion continues to be a prominent cause of division and tension between Christians and Hindus. Several Indian states have enacted legislation to prohibit conversions through coercion, allurement, and fraud. There are also calls for national anticonversion laws.

The state of Odisha (formerly Orissa) was the first to enact anticonversion legislation: the Orissa Freedom of Religion Act, 1967.[3] In the words of this act, "No person shall convert or attempt to convert, either directly or otherwise, any person from one religious faith to another by the use of force or by inducement or by any fraudulent means nor shall any person abet any such conversion." *Conversion* is defined as "renouncing one religion and adopting another," and the meaning of *force* includes "a show of force or a threat of injury of any kind, including the threat of divine displeasure or social excommunication." *Inducement* includes "the offer of any gift or gratification, either in cash or in kind, and shall also include the grant of any benefit, either pecuniary or otherwise." Finally, *fraud* is defined to include "misrepresentation or any other fraudulent contrivance." The provisions of the laws in other states are quite similar to the Odisha legislation. Although this bill and others like it do not make the act of converting from one religion to another illegal, consensus on the meaning of terms like *force*, *inducement*, and *fraudulent* is impossible. The threat of "divine displeasure," for example, is included in the definition of *force*, highlighting the deep differences over this matter.

Mission and the Sharing of Traditions

Hindus, on the whole, have the perception that mission is the single and most important concern of Christianity. They understand it to be a compulsion that is driven by the nature of exclusive Christian theological claims. The preamble to the CWMW begins with the affirmation that "mission belongs to the very being of the church. Proclaiming the word of God and witnessing to the world is essential for every Christian." Of course, the purpose of the document is to stipulate and describe the proper and appropriate ways in which such a mission may be conducted. The opening words of the CWMW, however, do not change the widespread Hindu view of mission as the primary concern of Christianity.

The Hindu tradition is not averse to the sharing of religious teaching and, in fact, commends such sharing. The often-cited Ṛg Veda (1.89.1) text, "Let noble truths come to us from all sides," expresses the deep and ancient Hindu value for sharing and receiving wisdom. At the conclusion of the Bhagavadgītā (18:67–71), the teacher, Krishna, commends the sharing of his teachings. He characterizes the sharing of wisdom as the dearest form of service and the teacher as dearest to him among human beings (18:69).

> One who reveals this supreme secret to those who
>   have offered me their love,
> Enacting the highest offering of love for me—that one
>   shall certainly come to me, without doubt.
> And among humans, there is no one whose acts are
>   more dearly loved by me than that one,
> Nor shall there be any other on earth who is more
>   dearly loved by me than such a person.[4]

The motivation for such sharing is the conviction that these teachings are universally relevant and conducive to human well-being. The sharer hopes that the consequence of such sharing is that others are persuaded to embrace these teachings by awakening to their truth and beauty. Swami Vivekananda (1863–1902) undertook the hazardous and pioneering journey from India to the United States in the late nineteenth century, inspired by the conviction that the message of the Vedānta tradition was needed by and good for persons in the West. His path continues to be followed by a line of distinguished Hindu teachers. Hindu traditions, therefore, are not unfamiliar with the religious motive of sharing one's conviction, debating, and persuading others about its validity.

Sharing in the Hindu tradition, however, occurred generally in response to a request for religious teaching made by a student to a teacher. It was always felt that this teaching spoke meaningfully to the person who had examined life's experiences and discovered that finite or created ends such as power, wealth, fame, or pleasure are ultimately unfulfilling. A religious need, in other words, must be established and not presumed. It is the function of the teacher to validate this need and to impart wisdom through words and personal examples. The qualified teacher is one who knows the sacred texts and methods of imparting wisdom and whose life is firmly rooted in what she teaches. Hindus regard religious teachers with profound respect and honor as exemplars of sacred teaching.

Religious teaching is liberating when shared by a qualified teacher to a receptive student who is devoted to ethical values, who practices self-control, and whose mind is focused. The dissemination and receipt of religious teaching is a demanding and transformative process that requires commitment and dedication as a disciple. Debates occurred among leaders of theological traditions, but the absence of institutionalization and centralization meant that there were no systematic efforts to supplant different viewpoints. Today, Hindus become uneasy and suspicious of grand plans, programs, and resources aimed at conversion and of the development of missionary strategies targeting particular religious communities. Such planned and programmatic efforts at conversion cause Hindus to feel under attack and lead to defensive attitudes.

A Different Starting Point?

Could we consider a starting point different from the preamble's affirmation of the centrality of mission for Christian identity?

The CWMW speaks importantly about mission being conducted with gentleness and respect in the context of dialogue: "Christians are called to conduct themselves with integrity, charity, compassion and humility, to overcome all arrogance, condescension and disparagement."[5] In the conduct of mission, Christians are advised that "this should be done ecumenically, and in consultation with representatives of other religions."[6] Bearing false witness against other religions is denounced, and appreciation for "what is true and good in them" is commended.[7]

Hindus would welcome these recommendations. I believe that practitioners of both traditions would not rest content with a passive tolerance that excluded engagement. We do not wish our traditions to be fortresses in which we live in isolation from our neighbors of other faiths. The CWMW assumes active engagement between Hindus and Christians characterized by mutual respect, learning in dialogue, and cooperation in the pursuit of justice, peace, and the common good.

Could there be a different starting point? Instead of mission, we may start, as Hindus and Christians, with the truth of the one divine reality who is the source of all life. The Upaniṣads—that is, the wisdom section of the Vedas—speak of God as "that from which all beings originate, by which they are sustained and to which they return" (Taittirīya Upaniṣad 3.1.1).[8] The Upaniṣads contest the existence of anything but the One God before creation and the emergence of the world from anything other than God. The Bhagavadgītā (9:17–18) speaks of God as father and mother of the universe and as its nourisher, lord, goal, and friend. God is not the national, tribal, or exclusive deity of a particular religious or ethnic community but the source of all life and existence. God is not Hindu or Christian.

In 1998, I was invited by the World Council of Churches to participate as a Hindu guest at its eighth assembly in Harare, Zimbabwe (December 3–14).[9] With guests of other faiths, we presented at a series of "padares."[10] One "padare" at which I spoke had the provocative title "My God, Your God, Our God, No God?" Speaking from a Hindu perspective, I suggested that "unless our understanding of the absolute is specifically tribal, ethnic or national in nature, we hold it to be the source, support and destiny of all beings. Where the absolute is understood as a personal God, God is understood as the creator of all beings and not just of a specific group. Our understanding of the absolute is such that it would be contradictory to propose that it could be anything other than one. God is clearly our God. The absolute One is not yours or mine, but ours. It does not belong to us; we belong to it."[11] The danger of overlooking the universal God of our traditions is tribalizing our understanding of God and limiting God to the boundaries of our communities and our concerns.

The Hindu affirmation of the truth of a universal divine one who is the source of all existence is not a theological footnote. For Mahatma Gandhi, the implication is unity and identity with the other. "I believe," wrote Gandhi, "in the absolute oneness of God and, therefore, of humanity."[12] With a common origin in the divine, human beings constitute a single family. According to the Maha Upaniṣad (6:71–72), only those with small minds distinguish between the relative and the stranger. For those who live generously, the entire world constitutes one family.[13]

Like the Upaniṣads, the Bible also begins with the origin of all from God. In the words of the Christian theologian S. Wesley Ariarajah, "Significantly it is the story not of the creation of the church, or of Christians, not even of Israel, but of the cosmos. 'In the beginning, God created the heavens and the earth.' This belief that God is the creator of everything and everybody is basic to the Bible. There is nothing that is outside God's providence; there is no life, no experience, no worship, no liberation, no salvation that can happen outside of the scope of God's love and knowledge."[14] From God's side, according to Ariarajah, echoing the beautiful Maha Upaniṣad text cited above, there can only be one family—the human family. The Īśa Upaniṣad (1) speaks of the universe as enfolded in God. Nothing and no one are outside of God; nothing exists separate from God. Enfolding is a form of embracing and suggests care and love. In the words of Rowan Williams, "God is the unique source of everything."[15]

The Upaniṣads, however, do not stop there. They teach that after bringing forth this wondrous diversity, the divine is present equally in every being; everyone and everything is enfolded most intimately in God. Nothing exists outside of God, and nothing exists but for the fact that it receives the gift of moment-to-moment sustenance from God.

Psalm 139 instructs about the encompassing divine reality rhetorically: "Where can I go from your spirit? Or where can I flee from your presence? If I ascend to heaven, you are there; if I make my bed in Sheol, you are there" (7–8 NRSV). In Acts 17:27–28, Paul reflects on the paradox of the human quest for God and cites a text some attribute to a Greek philosopher, Epimenides: "They would search for God and perhaps grope for him and find him—though indeed he is not far from each one of us. For 'In him we live and move and have our being'" (NRSV). Rowan Williams speaks of divine immanence in the language of divine action: "It means that within every circumstance, every object, every person, God's action is going on, a sort of white heat at the centre of everything."[16] In his version of the Rāmāyaṇa, the religious poet, Tulasidās, beautifully meditates on the paradox of God's immanence. In Ayodhyākāṇḍa (in the chapter on Ayodhya), Rama, God-incarnate for millions of Hindus, who is exiled in the forest, approaches the sage

Valmiki, inquiring about a suitable place to construct a new home. Valmiki's rhetorical reply is not unlike the question in Psalm 139: "You ask me, 'Where should I stay?' I ask you humbly to tell me where you do not exist; then I will show you a place."[17]

This truth of divinity abiding in all hearts is the most fundamental source and ground of the intrinsic dignity and equal worth of every human being. It is our theological antibody to the instrumentalization of human beings and the denial of their personhood. The implication, I want to suggest, for both Hindus and Christians, is that we cannot honor and value God and devalue human beings. We cannot give our assent or support to any social or cultural system that is founded on human inequality and indignity.

The positive implications of divine immanence are just as important as the rejection of inequality and injustice in structures such as casteism, racism, and sexism. The single value and practice that expresses best the meaning of Hindu spirituality is compassion (*dayā*). In Bhagavadgītā 12:13, Krishna describes the religious person who is dear to him as one who is free from hate and who is friendly, compassionate, and forgiving. It is important to underline that he speaks not just of freedom from hate (*adveṣṭā*) but, positively, of friendship (*maitraḥ*) and compassion (*dayā*). The saint-poet Tulasidās also gives pride of place to compassion as the expression of the religious life and describes it as being one with the other in suffering and happiness (*para duḥkha duḥkha sukha sukha*). He identifies the essence of ethics (*dharma*) with working for the well-being of others and its opposite (*adharma*) with oppression.[18]

For the great Protestant reformer Martin Luther, the religious life is a life of service. The meaning of service is enriched immeasurably by understanding that the "recipients of service are Christ incarnate within human need."[19] He invites Christian fathers to imagine holding the baby Jesus in their hands when changing the dirty diapers of their children. "I confess to thee," writes Luther, "that I am not worthy to rock this little babe or wash its diapers, or to be entrusted with the care of the child and its mother. How is it that I, without any merit, have come to this distinction of being certain that I am serving thy creature and thy most precious will?"[20]

The Limits of Our Knowing

Along with the teaching that all life originates from the one divine being and that this truth is expressed in relationships of compassion, Hindu traditions call attention to the limits of human understanding and language in relation to God. God is always more than can be defined, described, or understood by the finite human mind. This is the point of the often-quoted Ṛg Veda (1.64.46) text: "The One Being the wise speak of in many ways." The text is a comment on the finitude of all human language in relation to the absolute. In trying to describe it, language will be diverse, since the absolute exceeds all descriptions. Each word, each symbol is inadequate and reflects the historical and cultural conditions under which it occurs. The consequence is epistemological and theological humility. Hinduism reminds us that our discourse about God must not be absolutized and our symbols must not be confused with the reality to which these point. In relation to God, we must admit that our understanding always falls short.

The acknowledgment of the limits of language and the relativity of human experience preclude any Hindu claim to the ownership of truth in its fullness and finality. While firmly rooted in the view that the universe has its source and being in the One the Upaniṣads refer to as *brahman*, the tradition has consistently admitted that this One transcends all limited human efforts at definition and description. The Taittirīya Upaniṣad (2.9.1) speaks of *brahman* as "that from which all words, along with the mind, turn back, having failed to grasp." The Kena Upaniṣad (2:3) expresses the impossibility of ordinary ways of comprehending the infinite in the manner of a finite object. The text delights in the language of paradox: "It is known to him to whom It is unknown; he does not know It to whom It is Known. It is unknown to those who know well and known to those who do not know."

The point of such texts is not to demean human language or to negate the teachings of our traditions but to remind us of the limits of our understanding and symbols in relation to God. It is a central Hindu conviction that all words are inadequate and that the One is always more than we could define, describe, or understand with our finite minds.[21] This recognition of the intrinsic human limitation in attaining or formulating a complete knowledge of God means that no intellectual, theological, or iconic representation is ever full and final. Each one struggles to grasp and express that which is ultimately inexpressible, and each attempt reflects and is influenced by the cultural and historical conditions under which it occurs. Hindu traditions are *darśanas*, precious and distinctive ways of seeing and understanding, but in relation to the limitlessness of the One, no way of seeing can claim fullness of knowledge.

Such teachings are not unknown in Christianity. In the fourth century, Cyril of Jerusalem wrote, "We explain not what God is but candidly confess that we have not exact knowledge concerning Him. For in what concerns God, to confess our ignorance is best knowledge."[22] Pseudo-Dionysius is famous for his apophatic theology, but he felt that describing God through negation was presumptuous. Augustine commended "learned ignorance."[23]

Mutual Learning in Humility

If it is impossible to confine the One within the boundaries of our religion or to represent it entirely through the language of our theologies, we must consider the possibility of meaningful teachings from others that may open our hearts and minds to the inexhaustible nature of the divine. Our confession of the limits of human understanding and symbols provides a powerful justification for dialogical relationships of humility and reverence with persons of other traditions. Religious exclusivism and arrogance are the consequences of thinking that one has a privileged relationship with God or truth in its fullness. It is the outcome of limiting knowledge of God to one's community, sacred text, and place of worship.

Starting with the universality of the divine and the limits of human understanding and symbols requires that we conduct ourselves "with integrity, charity, compassion and humility" and that we strive "to overcome all arrogance, condescension and disparagement."[24]

Acknowledging the limits of our understanding is not the same as asserting relativistic generalizations about the sameness of all religious teachings and their moral equivalence. Although there are some Hindu interpreters who seem to suggest that religious differences are only semantic, the tradition does not advocate the sameness of religions or the equal validity of all teaching and practices. The Ṛg Veda (1.64.46) text quoted earlier, "The One Being the wise speak of in many ways," does offer the suggestion that religions speak differently about one reality but does not suggest that the different ways in which we speak are insignificant. It also does not mean that all ways of speaking are equally true and valid or that the ways that we speak make no difference. Surely, the ways in which we speak about the absolute are important, since these not only reveal our understanding of its nature but also provide moral guidance for our lives in the world.

By acknowledging that wise people speak differently about God, the text invites a respectful and inquiring response to religious diversity. We must not hastily and arrogantly denounce the sacred speech of the other as undeserving of sincere and serious contemplation. Wisdom must not be identified solely with our way of speaking, and we should not assume that wise persons always speak identically or that wisdom is manifested only in consensus.

Today, we are much more aware of ways of speaking in the name of God that awaken hate and instigate violence toward others within and outside our traditions. Some religious voices can legitimize injustice and oppression even as others can liberate and advocate for equality. It is naive and dangerous to attribute equal validity to all religious voices. Even Mahatma Gandhi, a great advocate of religious diversity, found it necessary to critique certain religious beliefs and practices. The great Hindu failure, in Gandhi's view, was untouchability, and he could not affirm interpretations of the tradition that sanctioned its demeaning practices. Mere differences in speech do not indicate wisdom, and we are not exempted from exercising discernment in choosing those ways of speaking about God that are conducive to the universal common good and human flourishing.

Acts of Service

CWMW principle 4 calls upon Christians to serve others through acts of service that include "providing education, health care, relief services, and acts of justice" that "are an integral part of witnessing to the gospel." These commendable and necessary acts of service, however, are sources of tension between Hindus and Christians. Many Hindus see such actions as part of the overall strategy of proselytization: "The objective of the social service is to get an access to the people who are targeted for conversion. Once the missionaries come close to the people, and the latter become obligated to them, the 'benefits' of believing in Christ are explained to them."[25]

There are several issues underlying this tension. The Hindu tradition has a deep value for service, and Hindus are encouraged to be generous in gifts to the needy. Chapter 17 of the Bhagavadgītā discusses appropriate and inappropriate ways of serving others. The text commends service that is motivated by a belief in the intrinsic value of serving, that is without expectation of reward, and that is offered to a needy person at a proper place and time. Less commendable is service that is reluctantly offered, with the aim of receiving something in return. When there is a link between social service and proselytization, Hindus are troubled by what is contrary to their tradition's emphasis on service without expectation of reward (*niṣkāmakarma*).

It is not true that all Christian acts of service are motivated by proselytization. Social service, inspired by the perspective of Christian liberation theology, is concerned less with conversion and more with the transformation of society through the practice of justice, the overcoming of suffering, and the transforming of structures of oppression. In those forms of Christianity that emphasize the role of Jesus as a social prophet and his criticism of systems of domination, liberation is construed, not only as the overcoming of estrangement from God, but also as liberation from systems of domination and the creation of a just and inclusive social order. Activity directed toward this end, such as the provision of education, health care, housing, food, and clothing, is seen by Christians as an inextricable expression of the meaning of their religious commitment and the quality of human relationships that this commitment requires. Hindus will benefit from dialogue with Christians about the meaning of liberation and the work to transform social systems.

CWMW principle 4 clearly states that the "exploitation of situations of poverty and need has no place in Christian outreach. Christians should denounce and refrain from offering all forms of allurements, including financial incentives and rewards, in their acts of service." This important statement needs to be publicized widely among Christians engaged in mission activity. Hindus and Christians could agree that it is wrong to use material rewards as means of enticing another to join one's religion. Meaningful faith is not awakened and nurtured by exploiting others in times of vulnerability and need. Hindus also need to refrain from sweeping generalizations about the significance of charitable works in the lives of Christians and to understand better why, under conditions of oppression and deprivation, the caring face of God attracts. There is a lot of Christian humanitarian work, both past and present, that is not linked to conversion, but this commendable expression of Christian values is made suspect by those who use works of charity to win converts.

This controversial matter can be addressed, in part, through Christians cooperating with people of other traditions in bringing relief to the poor and dispossessed. Such joint effort will build trust and help make the point that it is the overcoming of suffering and not conversion that is the primary concern of religious persons. Such shared work would be an eloquent expression of what it means to be Hindu and Christian in circumstances of suffering. Clearly, we need a more comprehensive understanding of the sources of human suffering and the role of religion in the midst of injustice and oppression. Both Hindus and Christians can benefit immensely from such a discussion and from common action.

Theology and Mission

The CWMW preamble makes a clarifying claim that "the document does not intend to be a theological statement on mission but to address practical issues associated with Christian witness in a multi-religious world." Although it is true that this document does not offer a systematic theology of mission or religions, there is much that is theological in this text. I noted earlier that the CWMW begins with the affirmation of the indispensability of mission. It affirms Jesus Christ as the supreme witness and the commission and responsibility to witness to him. This obligation to mission is clearly rooted in Christian theological claims in relation to persons of other traditions, and from this perspective, the CWMW is certainly not theologically neutral. If a particular Christian theology undergirds mission, should this theology not be transformed by the real and deep encounters with persons of other traditions that is commended in this document?

The CWMW commends dialogue: "Christians are to speak sincerely and respectfully; they are to listen in order to learn about and understand others' beliefs and practices and are encouraged to acknowledge and appreciate what is true and good in them."[26] It seems to me, however, that these most commendable practices of dialogue require one further step. It is not enough to commend learning from people of other traditions; the implications of such learning must also be considered. Through deep relationships with people of other traditions, so extensively commended in the CWMW, we will come to know of their claims to revelations, their affirmation of God's unity, and their profound relationships with God and the expression of this relationship in lives of compassion, generosity, and service. Surely such learning has implications, not merely for the ethics of mission, but for the very nature and purpose of mission. There is an evident tension between the call for dialogue and openness to learning and the primacy of mission. What is the significance of learning if it does not transform mission? Hindus experience uncertainty about the value of the Hindu tradition in the eyes of their Christian dialogue partners.

In a lecture to a group of Christian missionaries, Gandhi reminded them about the necessity of receiving as well as giving: "You cannot give without taking. If you have come to give rich treasures of experiences, open your hearts out to receive the treasures of this land, and you will not be disappointed, neither will you have misread the message of the Bible."[27] Meaningful learning from dialogue is never passive; that which we receive, if we acknowledge its worth, has to be meaningfully integrated with our deepest convictions. Such integration requires careful discernment.

Today, through dialogue, interpersonal friendships, and scholarship, we know more about the lives and faiths of our neighbors of other religions than at any time before. It would be sad if the culmination of this learning is theological neutrality and the unwillingness to reconsider the basic purpose of mission. What knowledge of people of other faiths do we need in order to move away from mission as the primary Christian obligation? What is the value of dialogue and deep relationships if, at the end of it all, there is no fundamental reconsideration of the purpose of mission?

In building relationships with people of other faiths, characterized by mutual respect and mutual giving and receiving in humility, the starting point does not have to be the imperative of mission. The constant pairing of evangelization with dialogue is not helpful for dialogue. When these two are treated as inseparable, it is only evangelization that is heard, given the reality of history. A suspicion about Christian intent impedes the development of trust. Is the Christian tradition betrayed by discourse about dialogue that does not equally affirm the commitment to evangelization? Alternative starting points ought to be the unity of the divine as the source of all life, the limits of human understanding, the unity of the human community, learning from one another in mutual respect and humility, and addressing together the causes of human suffering.

At the beginning of this chapter, I spoke of Swami Vivekananda, who came to the western world with the conviction that the Vedānta tradition, and in a special way the nondual (*Advaita*) teaching, had truths that were universally relevant and enriching for persons from the Christian tradition. He came to share these truths. In the course of doing so, many became disciples and crossed over into Vivekananda's tradition. Such crossing over as a consequence of mutual learning and sharing in dialogue is a real possibility that Hindus and Christians must acknowledge. I regard this, however, as different from having conversion at the center of all religious encounters.

Theological Resources and Challenges to Hindu-Christian Dialogue

In 1997 (October 23–27), nineteen Hindus and Christians from various parts of our world (India, Fiji, Canada, the United States, and Switzerland) met in Varanasi, India, for a Hindu-Christian consultation under the auspices of the World Council of Churches (Office of Interreligious Dialogue and Cooperation) and the National Council of Churches in India. The objective of the consultation was to discuss Hindu-Christian relations with the goal of a united world family (Towards One World Family—Ek Dharti Parivar Ki Ore).[1]

We talked about many of the topics discussed in this book. These included aggressive proselytization, religious extremism, caste discrimination, and the necessity to understand and respect the unique self-definitions in each tradition. We committed ourselves to continuing the work of building Hindu-Christian relationships through sharing publications, networking, and providing education. We identified topics for future consultations. These included mission and dialogue, Dalit discrimination, scripture, interpretation, and tradition. Regretfully, the hope and optimism with which we left the Varanasi consultation twenty-five years ago were, for various reasons, not sustained. As Hindus and Christians, we did not follow through on our commitments to work together to build an inclusive world family.

At this consultation in Varanasi, I was invited to give the keynote address. I divided my presentation using a number of significant questions: Are Hindus interested in dialogue with Christians? Is dialogue a Christian problem? Is there anything to discuss? Are there no differences? Is there anything to learn? Is there a future for Hindu-Christian dialogue? My aim in this chapter is to revisit these questions that I still regard as significant for the future of Hindu-Christian dialogue. I do not consider this list of questions to be comprehensive, and I recognize that other questions may be significant for Hindu and Christian communities in different parts of our world.

Are Hindus Interested in Dialogue with Christians?

Many have observed that Hindus exemplify little interest in dialogue with Christians. Klaus Klostermaier, for example, notes that "there are few Hindus who are interested in (contemporary) Christian theology, and there are fewer still who have a desire to enter into dialogue with their Christian counterparts."[2] In the words of Harold Coward, "Contemporary Hindu thinkers do not seem to be engaged with Christianity in the same way their predecessors were at the turn of the century (for example, Roy, Sen, Dayananda and Radhakrishnan)."[3] Others have made similar observations. Margaret Chatterjee laments that the interest shown by Hindu reformers in the nineteenth and early twentieth centuries has not been sustained.[4] It remains true that, with few notable exceptions, the initiatives for dialogue have been from the Christian side.

These commentators, I want to suggest, do not imply that Hindus are uninterested in dialogue with Christians and people of other religious traditions. The suggestion is that Hindus are not active promoters of organized interreligious dialogue. They are generally willing participants in interreligious dialogue but are not always the initiators.

This observation is still largely true for many reasons. Hinduism continues to be a decentralized religious tradition. Its leadership is largely individual in nature, and it has not developed institutional structures similar to Christianity. Its authoritative voices are many, and it is often slower to identify, analyze, and respond to contemporary challenges. The traditions of Hinduism have not generated formal statements about the theological significance of other traditions and the purposes of interreligious dialogue. Given the absence of central organizations and decision-making processes, it is difficult to see how such statements would emerge.[5] The resources for dialogue that we have in the Hindu tradition are articulated by individual Hindu leaders like Gandhi or Swami Vivekananda.[6] It is possible that, with the growth of umbrella-type Hindu organizations, especially outside of the Indian subcontinent, we will see more institutional dialogue initiatives among Hindus and even formal statements about relationships with other religions. At the present time, umbrella-type organizations like the Hindu Acharya Dharma Sabha or the Vishwa Hindu Parishad (World Hindu Assembly) do not give prominence to dialogue with other traditions. Even the Hindu American Foundation in the United States does not list interreligious relationships as a goal.

It is also true, as I noted earlier, that most Hindus continue to see Christianity as a tradition that is concerned exclusively with conversion. They think of Christianity as an exclusive religion that is not genuinely open to the religious claims and experiences of others and that is concerned primarily with increasing its institutional power and domination through evangelization and conversion. Ashok Chowgule, vice president of the influential Vishwa Hindu Parishad, summarized what most Hindus think of Christianity:

Christianity believes in exclusivism. It says that Christ is the only Son of God and was sent to this world to lead the people to him. Upon the death of Christ, this task was given to the Church set up in the name of Christ. The present inheritors of Christ are the Popes, the Cardinals, the Bishops, the priests, etc. Furthermore, Christianity believes that Christ has commanded his followers that it is their duty to convert others to their system. Many have interpreted this command to imply that one could use physical violence as a means to achieve the objective.[7]

I believe that Hindus are still suspicious that interreligious dialogue is a new instrument for evangelization. When words like *evangelization, proclamation,* and *mission* are used repeatedly with *dialogue,* these terms are the ones that stand out in the Hindu mind. Can Christians speak of dialogue without speaking of evangelization? Methodist theologian and interreligious dialogue pioneer S. Wesley Ariarajah articulated well this predicament for Hindus: "Neighbors of other faiths, therefore, receive mixed signals. While groups of Christians appear to be advocating an open, genuinely mutual and trusting relationship committed to the creation of a community of communities that would live in peace with each other and in mutual witness, other groups are bent on converting them to Christ. . . . It would appear that each time a Hindu meets with a Christian, he or she must ask, 'Which mood are you in?' (mission or dialogue) before deciding whether to continue."[8]

In chapter 3, I discuss the rise of Hindu nationalism (Hindutva). Vinayak Damodar Savarkar, the systematizer of the ideology of Hindutva, contended that Hindus were the original Indigenous people of India and constituted one single nation. Hindus constitute not only a nation but also a race (*jāti*) with a common origin, blood, and culture. Savarkar defined Hindus as those who consider India as their holyland (*puṇyabhūmi*) and the land of their ancestors (*pitṛibhūmi*). In Savarkar's view, Sikhs, Jains, and South Asian Buddhists are Hindus. Savarkar names their common culture as Sanskriti, on the basis of the claim that Sanskrit is the language that expresses and preserves all that is worthy in the history of the Hindus. It includes a shared history, literature, art, law, festivals, rites, rituals, and heroes. This criterion was the basis for his exclusion of Indian Christians. Despite sharing territory and blood, they had, in Savarkar's words, "ceased to own Hindu civilization (Sanskriti) as a whole. They belong or feel that they belong to a cultural unit altogether different from the Hindu one."[9]

It is not difficult to understand how such an attitude to the Christian community in India is a significant impediment to interreligious dialogue and relationships, since it encourages hostility and exclusion. It is imperative for Hindus who are committed to building relationships with Christian communities and working together for the common good to challenge the ideology of Hindutva by drawing deeply from the rich resources of the tradition for hospitality and the celebration of religious diversity. It is important to understand that Hindutva is not just an innocuous expression of commitment to Hinduism or pride in one's religious and cultural heritage. It is fundamentally an ideology of exclusion and marginalization of those who do not satisfy Savarkar's definition of legitimate Indian national identity. Demanding that our dialogue partners redefine themselves as a condition of participation and acceptance is unjust and a flawed requirement for dialogue. The growth of Hindu nationalism is one of the many factors discouraging Hindu interest in dialogue with Christians.

Is Dialogue a Christian Theological Problem?

Related to my discussion above is a widespread Hindu perception that interreligious dialogue is a special Christian problem because Christianity, among all the world's religions, is most challenged theologically by the fact of religious diversity. There is no doubt that the Christian tradition has come to feel the theological challenges of religious diversity more keenly than other religions and has been wrestling to find new ways to define itself in relation to these traditions.[10] This has to do with the exclusive nature of the traditional Christian claim that Jesus Christ is the unique and universal savior of the world and that there is salvation through no other. Exclusive claims about God and revelation ought to be reexamined when we encounter people outside of our traditions in whose life and work the love and grace of God are manifest. It is also not true that exclusivism is the sole Christian theological response to other religions.

If theologies of exclusivism and inclusivist theologies that propose one religion to be fulfillment of all others are challenged by the reality of religious diversity, these challenges certainly extend also to the Hindu tradition. Swami Dayananda Saraswati (1824–83), for example, founder of the reformist Arya Samaj, took his stand on the Vedas that he understood to be the infallible repository of all knowledge, secular and sacred. On the basis of his interpretations of the Vedas, he launched a vigorous attack on Jainism, Buddhism, Islam, and especially Christianity. He thought of the Christian tradition as standing or falling on the authority of the Bible. In his major work, *Satyartha Prakash* (*Light of Truth*), Saraswati sought to show that the contents of the Bible are immoral, untrue, and irrational.[11] In Swami Dayananda Saraswati, there is none of the esteem and respect for Jesus that is generally found in Hindu religious teachers. He challenges the Christian understanding of Jesus as the Son of God, the truth of the miracles ascribed to him, his resurrection from the grave, and the doctrine of atonement. Christians, according to Saraswati, were inconsistent in arguing for the miracles of Jesus while denying such claims in the Hindu tradition. Jesus, in Saraswati's view, is not a person who offers valuable religious teachings to Hindus and cannot serve as an exemplar of ethics.

A theology of inclusivism was articulated by Swami Bhaktivedanta (1896–1977), founder of the International Society for Krishna Consciousness. While he acknowledged truths in other religions, he understood them to be all incomplete. The sure way to liberation is the path of *bhakti* (devotion) to Krishna. Swami Bhaktivedanta, according to R. D. Baird, proposes that "if one is to return to Godhead, one must finally resort to *bhakti*, which alone raises one above the mundane plane to the transcendental level. While one's goal is not to convert people to 'Hinduism,' Krishna consciousness is not 'Hinduism' but represented as *sanātana dharma* or the eternal religion."[12] There are other Hindu teachers and leaders who advocated for more pluralistic theologies of religion. These include Mahatma Gandhi and Sri Ramakrishna, the teacher of Swami Vivekananda.[13]

There can be little doubt that the Hindu tradition offers important resources for our understanding of religious diversity.[14] The tradition, however, is not homogenous in this regard. I make mention of diverse theologies of religion in the Hindu tradition to emphasize the point that the challenges of religious pluralism are not limited to Christianity. As Hindus, we cannot be critical of exclusivist theologies in other traditions without acknowledging versions in our own. Religious diversity challenges us all theologically, and dialogue between our traditions is an important resource for mutual learning. There are wonderful insights in Hinduism for interpreting and explaining religious pluralism, but Hindus cannot assume that the tradition has resolved theologically all the dilemmas of religious diversity.

Is There Anything to Discuss?

In April 1997, I was invited by the United States Catholic Conference of Bishops to discuss plans for initiating a program of Catholic-Hindu dialogue in the United States. We met at the University of Saint Mary of the Lake/Mundelein Seminary in Illinois. I have a vivid recollection of the contribution of one of my fellow Hindu participants who argued strongly that the fundamental basis of the Hindu tradition is mystical experience (*anubhava*) and not scriptural teachings. In my colleague's view, interreligious dialogue is appropriate only to religious traditions that value teachings derived from a scripture; such claims are absent in Hinduism. Christianity, he argued, is a doctrine-based tradition, and dialogue is more appropriate and useful to such a tradition. Dialogue, as a mode of relating to other traditions, he implied, does not fit Hinduism.

This argument was familiar and interesting to me, since I had studied the significance of the authority of scripture in the commentaries of the classical Hindu theologian Śaṅkara for my doctoral dissertation.[15] I had also published a book on the growing significance of mystical experience in contemporary Hinduism.[16] Religious experience is indeed a vital part of Hindu spirituality, but it was not always championed at the expense of the life of the intellect and reason or independent of sacred teachings and texts. The prominence that is given in contemporary Hinduism to mystical experience is connected, I believe, to a decline in the significance of scriptural, especially Vedic, exegesis and the reinterpretation of the authority of the Vedas. This has led, in my view, to a weakening of scholarship in Hinduism and in a lack of interest in dialogue with other traditions. It is not possible here to describe in detail and to trace the historical roots of this process of reinterpretation, and I have already attempted this elsewhere.[17]

I believe that the championing of the supremacy of personal mystical experience has contributed to the growing divorce of scholarship and spirituality. Examples of scholarship without religious commitment and of religious commitment lacking the self-critical insights of scholarship abound. Their creative combination in modern Hinduism is rare. The disconnection between scholarship and spirituality in Hinduism limits the quality of the Hindu dialogue with Christianity. The dialogue is particularly enriching when it occurs among participants whose lives reflect the creative integration of scholarship and spirituality.

S. Wesley Ariarajah identifies four different types of inter-religious dialogue, each with its unique contribution to make. A dialogue of life is the encounter that takes place in the course of everyday life among people of different traditions who live in the same community. In such encounters, the purpose is not a conscious or explicit articulation and exchange of religious belief. Conversations may be centered on family, work, or school, to give a few examples. The explicit exchange of beliefs and perspectives is a characteristic of the dialogue of discourse that has a more organized and formal character. In the dialogue of spirituality, participants seek "to go beyond words to encounter the other at the level of the heart." It attracts those "who feel that the essential unity of humanity cannot be expressed in words but must be celebrated in worship and meditation." Finally, the dialogue of action is characterized by cooperation among people of different faiths for the attainment of desirable ends for their common existence, such as peace, justice, protection of the environment, and human rights.[18]

What Ariarajah calls the dialogue of discourse must be important to Hindu-Christian dialogue. The sharing of wisdom, the understanding of the scope and limits of reason and language, and the mutual enrichment that comes from exposure to each other's teachings are facets of dialogue that, if engaged in with commitment, humility, and a passion for truth, can never become "ivory tower" intellectualism. Such dialogue needs to find a central place in the relationship of Hinduism and Christianity. A prominent scholar of Hinduism, Klaus Klostermaier, also laments the trend in contemporary Christianity and Hinduism "to dismiss the intellectual approach to religion as irrelevant and to cultivate only its emotional and pragmatic sides." Arguing that intellectuals and scholars must be allowed to play a more vital and central role in the development of these traditions, Klostermaier affirms that Hindu-Christian dialogue "must recover the intellectual substance of Hinduism and Christianity and must contribute actively to the ongoing search for truth/reality in all spheres of life. The intellectual dimension of life has not lost its importance in our time."[19]

When we look at the approach of classical Hindu theologians like Śaṅkara and Rāmānuja, we note the deep significance that they gave to the proper interpretation and understanding of sacred texts. Clearly, they did not treat doctrinal matters as being irrelevant or nonessential. They took doctrinal differences seriously and sought to understand the challenges of rival views and to offer appropriate responses. They meticulously presented and responded to different interpretations and worldviews. Of course, their approach was much more in the nature of debate than dialogue, and the concern for victory in argument was central to their motivation. I believe that the recovery and encouragement of this historical tradition of study, exegesis and engagement, would enrich Hindu-Christian dialogue in our own times.[20]

The downplaying of scriptural exegesis has other important implications for Hindu-Christian dialogue. One is the tendency to overlook the significance of doctrinal differences. Because conclusive insight is understood to be gained through mystical experience that transcends rational processes, it is easy to dismiss differences as preoccupations of the rational mind. However, such scant regard for differences of doctrine is often frustrating for many Christians who engage with Hindus in dialogue. Doctrine and discourse are not redundant, and differences are not unimportant. Although we must, in humility, hesitate to absolutize any discourse about the divine and not confuse the language symbols that we use with the reality to which these symbols point, we must take differences very seriously and not trivialize these as just semantic in nature.

The lament of Klostermaier is one that both of our traditions would do well to heed and address: "Intellectuals are not the favorite children of Mother Church in our time and age. Not only does one often have the impression that church leadership is not intellectual itself, it often comes through as anti-intellectual. There is a tendency to equate church membership with blind obedience to authority, faith with repetition of traditional formulae, theology with language regulation. There are true scholars within the church—but more than not they feel repressed, unwanted, under suspicion. In contemporary organized Hinduism too, the trend appears to be toward the political rather than toward the intellectual, toward agitation more than toward reflection."[21] The rise and spread of Hindu nationalism has confirmed Klostermaier's concerns.

Is There Anything to Learn?

Meaningful and deep dialogue thrive with appreciative knowledge of each other's tradition. Such knowledge is the fruit of patient study and inquiry. In this matter, however, there is an evident disparity. There are fewer Hindu scholars of Christianity than Christian scholars who study the Hindu tradition. In his response to the recently published *The Routledge Handbook of Hindu-Christian Relations*, Francis Clooney rightly notes that "a high proportion of the volume's contributors are of the Christian background, and a majority are academics living in Europe or the United States."[22] As Clooney notes, it is an unevenness that the editors are aware of and seek, in various ways, to address in the volume.

The reasons for this troubling scholarly discrepancy are many. It is true that the Christian interest in the study of other religious traditions was driven, in part, by the missionary enterprise, and there are still many Christian theological schools and seminaries where Hinduism and other religions are taught in the context of missiology. Today, however, the missionary motive is not the only one behind the study of other religions, and this needs to be acknowledged by Hindus. There are many scholars with Christian commitments who have dedicated themselves to the study of Hinduism and who have written about Hinduism in appreciative ways that committed Hindus could recognize. Their contributions to the scholarly study and teaching of the Hindu tradition must be acknowledged. Many of these are prominently involved in the dialogue with Hindus, and their understanding of the tradition is a great asset. I have mentioned several in this book, including S. Wesley Ariarajah, Diana Eck, Francis Clooney, and Klaus Klostermaier. There are many others who could be added. It is not easy, however, to identify Hindu scholars who undertake similar work on the Christian tradition. This fact is a significant one and constitutes an impediment to Hindu-Christian dialogue. I am encouraged, however, by the fact that there is an increasing number of students of Hindu background in graduate religion programs in the United States, Canada, the United Kingdom, and Europe. I believe that these graduates will contribute in the coming years to Hindu-Christian dialogue. On this point, I must disagree here with Klaus Klostermaier, who believed that Hindu-Christian dialogue in the West is pointless because of the doctrinally liberal character of Hinduism outside of India.[23] I believe that significant constructive developments in Hindu-Christian dialogue will occur outside of India as well.

There are also more pragmatic reasons for Hindu disinterest in the study of Christianity. There are very few opportunities outside of Indian seminaries and theological schools for the study of Christian theology in India and fewer employment opportunities for Hindu scholars who have expertise in Christianity. I believe that there is also reluctance on the part of many Hindus to undertake a serious study of Christianity that is still associated in Hindu minds with the history of colonialization and proselytization. Hindu nationalism, as I noted earlier, has also contributed to hostility toward Christians.

We must, however, also confront the possibility that the lack of Hindu interest in Christianity reflects the unfortunate belief that Hindus may not have much, if anything, to learn from Christianity. Let me cite the view of a Hindu participant in a Hindu-Christian dialogue meeting: "There can be only one Mother and mother may have many children. All these religions (children) can be categorized into three: Religions of Faith (ritual and worship); Religions of Love (Service and Self-sacrifice); Religions of Reason (discrimination and self-realization). Faith, Love and Reason are but the components of mankind irrespective of their effectiveness and intensity. The one religion (Mother) that has all of them in full is the whole and wholesome religion, unique and universal religion, accommodative and assimilating religion, complete and comprehensive religion, ancient and all-embracing religion. It is called Hinduism or Sanathana Dharma."[24] In addition to the fact that this statement overgeneralizes the world's religions, the characterization of Hinduism as the mother of all religions could be read as an argument against dialogue. In other words, since all religions are contained within the Hindu tradition, there is nothing new to learn outside.

There is also still a widespread view that religious differences are merely sematic. Such a view also contributes to disinterest in the possibilities of interreligious learning. The famous Ṛg Veda text "Ekam sat viprāh bahudhā vadanti" (I.164.46; "The One Being the wise speak of in many ways") is cited often by Hindus in interreligious contexts to minimize the significance of differences within and among religious traditions. I have argued against such interpretations of this important text and for the enriching significance of differences:

> Instead of seeing this text as underplaying differences, we may read from it the necessity for attentiveness to diverse ways of speaking about God. It is the wise (*viprāh*), after all, who speak differently about God. Theological diversity is not dismissed here as the consequence of ignorance. By acknowledging that wise people may speak differently about God, the text invites a respectful and inquiring response to religious diversity. We must not hastily and arrogantly denounce the sacred speech of the other as undeserving of sincere and serious contemplation. Wisdom must not be identified solely with our way of speaking and we should not assume that wise persons always speak identically or that wisdom is manifested only in consensus.[25]

Unfortunately, most Hindus continue to associate the Christian tradition with proselytization, biblical fundamentalism, the sinfulness of humanity, and faith in Jesus as being the only way to salvation. The rich heritage of theological and philosophical thought in Christianity remains unknown, even among Christians. There is also a deep heritage of mystical theology in Christianity that will be of interest to Hindu scholars but that is not prominent in Christian religious discourse. A work like the anonymously authored *The Cloud of Unknowing* and the teachings of the Cappadocian Fathers (Gregory of Nyssa, Basil of Caesarea, and Gregory of Nazianzus) and more recent figures like Meister Eckhart and Thomas Merton would provide wonderful resources for Hindu-Christian dialogue. One enduring contribution to Hindu-Christian dialogue would be the creation of opportunities for interested Hindu scholars to study the great works of Christian theology at institutions of Christian learning. A body of Hindu scholars with expertise in both traditions and an interest in dialogue would be a tremendous asset to the development of Hindu-Christian dialogue.

Is There a Future for Hindu-Christian Dialogue? A Model for Consideration

For almost a decade, beginning in 1999, a small group of Muslims, Buddhists, Hindus, Jews, and Christians met under the auspices of the World Council of Churches for a series of dialogue meetings that we named "Thinking Together." Rev. Dr. Hans Ucko, then program executive of the Office of Interreligious Relations and Dialogue of the World Council of Churches, was our dialogue convener for this novel gathering. The impetus for our meeting came from the recognition that we had always done most of our theological thinking without direct dialogue with our neighbors of other traditions. Could we think with and in the company persons of other faiths? How would our theological thinking be challenged and enriched by such dialogue?[26]

We were, in many ways, a privileged group. The generosity of the World Council of Churches made our meetings possible, but we exercised freedom in choosing the content and method of our discussions. There was no predetermined outcome that we felt obligated to generate. In addition, our freedom was enhanced by the fact that we were not participating as official representatives of our traditions. One of our participants,

Thomas Thangaraj, described our identities in these words: "Our accountability was to one another, even though we were quite conscious of our commitment and responsibility to our own religious communities. Therefore, religions were not in conversation; but practitioners and thinkers of various traditions were. It was not a dialogue among systems and institutions, but rather an encounter of minds, a dialogue of hearts, and a conversation of souls with an experience of true religious freedom."[27]

Whatever the topic we chose, our methodology was similar. We started with presentations on the topic at hand (e.g., violence, religious plurality, the other, conversion), ensuring that we heard different voices from each tradition and avoiding the homogenization of traditions. Each presentation was followed by responses from other traditions. They included questions, criticisms, and challenges as well as words of appreciation. There were times when we came to shared conclusions, and there were times when such shared conclusions were difficult. For example, after our discussions on "the other," we wrote, together, a series of shared conclusions.[28]

Since our meetings stretched over a number of years, we developed relationships that have endured over these decades. We became friends. We shared meals, went for walks, attended worship and meditation sessions led by members of our different traditions, and talked about our families. Our friendships blossomed to include trust, and our relationships became safe spaces where we could be vulnerable with one another, "sharing the joys and sorrows, ecstasies and agonies, successes and failures, and the beauty and ugliness of each of our religious traditions. We were willing, as well, to expose our ignorance of other's religious traditions."[29] Trust allowed us to be self-critical, a fundamental requisite for meaningful dialogue. We could drop our self-defensive barriers and acknowledge the ways in which all our traditions, at various times in history, legitimized structures of oppression and injustice and marginalized our fellow human beings. With the searchlight of history, we avoided the tendency to speak of the ideals of our traditions and the historical realities of others. We looked at our sacred texts and traditions in historical contexts.

Friendship and trust enabled us to cross what Diana Eck spoke of as the "terra incognita on the map of interreligious dialogue."[30] What Eck is referring to here is the journey from self-criticism to mutual criticism. "Both within and between traditions," writes Eck, "criticism must finally be safe and accepted if there is to be relationship and if knowledge of one another is to be more than superficial."[31] We crossed this terra incognita in our questions about caste, violence, proselytization, and claims about privileged relationships with the divine. Our discussions were difficult and often tense. Yet, with one exception after a very intense discussion, we did not retreat from dialogue, and we remained friends.

On this point, the example of Mahatma Gandhi is noteworthy. Gandhi recognized the importance and necessity of mutual questioning and criticism in dialogue. Without such freedom, dialogue runs the risk of being shallow and superficial. Gandhi expected his friends from other religions to be critical of him, and he invited their criticism. He understood also that such questioning required the cultivation of a relationship of trust. Trust is the soil in which truth can flourish and where the difficult questions that we want to ask one another can be raised. When relationships are characterized by historical suspicions and mistrust, mutual criticism may not be the appropriate starting point, and trust has to be nurtured first.

Gandhi reminds us that interreligious friendships do not require that we dispose of our deepest values and the theological commitments that serve as our norms for decision-making. The nature and sources of our theological and ethical criteria must be explicitly articulated, and we cannot entirely avoid conversations about justice and injustice, oppression and liberation, and casteism and racism. Interreligious friendships allow us to be questioned and to question our practices and understandings of ethical obligations. Identity with the other is deepened when it permits such mutual questioning and opens up the possibility for ethical growth and transformation. Very often, the injustices of our traditions are revealed to us only through the eyes and words of others. Their historical experiences and questions help us change, grow, and be more faithful to the heart of our own traditions.

Gandhi, however, believed that the right to criticize another tradition had to be earned. One had to first befriend the other and to show reverence for all that is good in other traditions. In one of his well-known statements, Gandhi spoke of the "duty of every cultured man or woman to read sympathetically the scriptures of the world. If we are to respect others' religions, as we would have them respect our own, a friendly study of the world's religions is a sacred duty."[32] One should seek understanding of other traditions by also pondering the writings of those who are practitioners of those traditions. Our "Thinking Together" experience, as described by Thangaraj, reflected and embodied, in so many ways, Gandhi's vision: "Without the development of friendship with one another, without a trust in one another's commitment to the common good, and without experiencing sheer delight in the presence of the other, one cannot engage in the kind of multifocal method we are referring to here. We were fortunate to be part of this story and engage in this method."[33]

We were fortunate indeed. Our dialogue is one form of interreligious engagement, but I describe it in detail here because I think that it offers us hope and direction for the future of Hindu-Christian dialogue. I believe that it could be creatively adapted and replicated at the local level by small groups of Hindus and Christians who appreciate the necessity, in our times, for building relationships of trust and care with each other.

Eboo Patel, drawing from the work of various social scientists who study religion, summarizes the three requirements for building relationships across religious differences.[34] He names these as attitudes, relationships, and knowledge. Relationships with people of other traditions and appreciative knowledge of those traditions results in positive attitudes. Where relationships are absent and knowledge lacking, attitudes are generally negative. Our "Thinking Together" dialogue succeeded because, as a deep process, it nurtured healthy relationships, empathetic understanding, and positive identity with one another's humanity. At the same time, going beyond Patel, our relationships matured with self-criticism and mutual criticism. This is my hope for the future of Hindu-Christian dialogue.

CHAPTER THREE

Hindu Nationalism (Hindutva) and Hindu-Christian Dialogue

> For those who live generously, the entire
> world constitutes a single family.
>
> —Maha Upaniṣad 6:71–72 (my translation)

Some years ago, a controversy erupted in India when the former Jammu and Kashmir chief minister, Omar Abdullah, protested against being forced to recite the slogan "Bharat Mata Ki Jai (Victory to Mother India)." The chanting of this slogan was promoted by Mohan Bhagwat, leader of the Rashtriya Swayamsevak Sangh (National Volunteer Organization), founded in 1925 to promote Hindu unity and service to the nation of India.[1] Many came forward to condemn Abdullah. Anupam Kher, a popular Bollywood actor, argued that the slogan defined nationalism.[2] Devendra Fadnavis, the chief minister of Maharashtra, claimed that those who were unwilling to chant the words had no right to Indian citizenship.[3] Uttar Pradesh Legislative Assembly member Surendra Singh declared that those who refused to say "Bharat Mata Ki Jai" are Pakistanis, have no right to reside in India, and should be debarred from political participation.[4] The Muslim community in India seems divided over this issue. Some see the slogan as expressing love for one's country that is not forbidden in Islam. Others, however, understand it to be a deification of the nation and a form of idolatry that Islam prohibits. Christians also seem to be divided over this issue.[5]

Vinayak Damodar Savarkar: A Definition of Indian Identity

The contemporary controversy surrounding this slogan, and especially its use as a test of loyalty to the nation, is only one of the more recent eruptions of a deep division and debate, going back to colonial times, around the issue of Indian identity. Who qualifies as an Indian? One of the earliest and most influential attempts to offer a definition of Indian national identity came from Vinayak Damodar Savarkar (1883–1966).[6] Savarkar expounded his ideology of Indian national identity in a small book titled *Hindutva: Who Is a Hindu? Hindutva* is an abstract noun formed by appending the Sanskrit masculine *tva* to *Hindu* and can be loosely translated as "Hinduness." Written while Savarkar was jailed in the Andaman Islands and subsequently in Ratnagiri by the British and published in 1923, *Hindutva* became the source of the principles that shaped the ideology of Hindu nationalism in the 1920s. Today, the term is widely employed to describe various expressions of the Hindu nationalist movement.

Although Savarkar uses the term *Hindutva*, he is essentially outlining the requirements of a broader Indian national identity. He himself did not profess a religious commitment, but his definition, as we will see, does have a significant religious dimension. His preference for the term *Hindutva* should not be construed as indicative only of a religious definition. In his book, he employs the name *Hindusthan* for India. Both of these names, Hindusthan and India, have a geographical origin and connectedness with the Indus River. *Hindu* is a Persian variation in the pronunciation of the name of the Indus River. It was a geographical term before it was used to denote a religious community, and Savarkar's use is geographical. It is important to note that for Savarkar, the terms *Hindu* and *Indian* are synonymous.

Citizenship

Savarkar's criteria for Hindu identity consist of three interrelated attributes. The first is geographical. India—or Hindusthan, as Savarkar would prefer to call it—constitutes a distinct geographical entity demarcated by mountains, oceans, and rivers, and a Hindu is "primarily a citizen, either in himself or through his forefathers, of 'Hindusthan.'"[7] On the basis of this first criterion, argues Savarkar, an American who becomes a citizen of Hindusthan is entitled to be treated as a countryman. However, he will not be incorporated into the Hindu fold if he does not satisfy the second requisite of Hinduness, since the term *Hindu* means much more than citizenship in India.

Common Ancestry

This second requirement of Hinduness is what Savarkar refers to as "common blood," or *jāti*. A Hindu is a descendant of Hindu parents and shares with other Hindus common blood traceable to the Vedic fathers or Sindhus. This argument rests essentially on an intuitive or affective claim: "We are not only a nation but a jati, a born brotherhood. Nothing else counts, it is after all a question of the heart. We feel that the same ancient blood that coursed through the veins of Ram and Krishna, Buddha and Mahavir, Nanak and Chaitanya, Basava and Madhava, of Rohidas and Tiruvelluvar courses throughout Hindudom from vein to vein, pulsates from heart to heart. We feel we are a jati, a race bound together by the dearest ties of blood and therefore it must be so."[8]

On the basis of the first two criteria of Hinduness, Christian and Muslim citizens of India may indeed be considered Hindus, since they are citizens and descendants of common ancestors. This was a possibility recognized by Savarkar, and what he writes here about Indian Muslims applies equally to Christians: "The majority of the Indian Mohammedans may, if free from the prejudices born of ignorance, come to love our land as their fatherland, as the patriotic and noble-minded amongst them have always been doing. The story of their conversions, forcibly in millions of cases, is too recent to make them forget, even if they like to do so, that they inherit Hindu blood in their veins. But can we, who are here concerned with investigating into facts as they are and not as they should be recognize these Mohammedans as Hindus?"[9]

Sanskriti Culture and India as Holyland

Savarkar answers his own question negatively by proposing a third criterion of Hinduness. This is the tie of homage to Hindu culture or civilization. Savarkar names this common culture as *Sanskriti* on the basis of the claim that Sanskrit is the language that expresses and preserves all that is worthy in the history of the Hindus. It includes a shared history, literature, art, law, festivals, rites, rituals, and heroes. This criterion was the basis for his exclusion not only of Indian Muslims but also of Indian Christians. These groups had, in Savarkar's words, "ceased to own Hindu civilization (Sanskriti) as a whole. They belong, or feel that they belong, to a cultural unit altogether different from the Hindu one."[10]

Savarkar was well aware of the existence of certain syncretistic communities in India, such as the Muslim Bohras and Khojas of Gujarat who incorporated many elements of Sanskriti culture into their daily lives. In order to exclude such groups from his definition, he turned, quite late in his text, to a consideration of the religious dimension of Hinduness. Hinduism or Hindu dharma includes all of the religious traditions, Vedic and non-Vedic, that originate from the soil of India. While the majority of Hindus subscribe to what is denoted as Sanatana dharma or Vaidik dharma, other traditions having roots in India such as Jainism, Sikhism, and Buddhism must be included in the generic category of Hinduism or Hindu dharma. All of these traditions, in Savarkar's view, look upon India not only as fatherland or motherland (*pitṛbhūmi*/*mātṛbhūmi*) but also as holyland (*puṇyabhūmi*). This is where the religious and the political intersect in Savarkar's Hindutva and where he finds his justification for excluding Indian Muslims and Christians:

> For though Hindusthan to them is Fatherland as to any other Hindu yet it is not to them a Holyland too. Their Holyland is far off in Arabia or Palestine. Their mythology and Godmen, ideas and heroes are not the children of this soil. Consequently, their names and their outlook smack of foreign origin. Their love is divided. Nay, if some of them be really believing what they profess to do, then there can be no choice—they must, to a man, set their Holyland above their fatherland in their love and allegiance. That is but natural. We are not condemning nor are we lamenting. We are simply telling facts as they stand. We have tried to determine the essentials of Hindutva and in doing so we have discovered that the Bohras and such other Mohammedan or Christian communities possess all the essential qualifications of Hindutva but one and that is that they do not look upon India as their Holyland.[11]

Savarkar's criteria help us understand better the significance of the controversy over the slogan "Bharat Mata Ki Jai." One's willingness to publicly recite these words is seen by Hindu nationalists as indicative of a regard for the nation as a holyland. It is significant that on February 26, 2003, amid controversy, a portrait of Savarkar was unveiled in the Central Hall of the Indian Parliament across from the portrait of Mahatma Gandhi.

Hinduism and Hindutva

One of the important distinctions made by Savarkar is between Hinduism and Hindutva. *Hinduism* is only the "ism" of the Hindu and refers specifically to the system of religious belief and practice. *Hindu*, on the other hand, refers to the territorial, "racial," and cultural factors constituting the Hindu nation. For Savarkar, one cannot determine the character of Hinduism without first defining who is a Hindu. Hindutva, for Savarkar, constitutes the unifying sociocultural background of all Hindus. In Savarkar's view, as noted above, Sikhs, Jains, and South Asian Buddhists are Hindus. By defining a Hindu as one who regards India as both fatherland and holyland, Savarkar excludes East Asian Buddhists, Western converts to Hinduism, and most importantly, Indian Muslims and Christians. For Savarkar, Muslims and Christians were essentially alien communities in India. Obviously, meaningful dialogue between Hindus and Christians is not possible as long as Christians are perceived to be alien communities in India and have their national commitments questioned. Dialogue requires affirmation of the religious identity and the right of self-definition of our dialogue partners.

To search for the unifying elements in a diverse nation is not inherently problematic. This is an ongoing project in many countries. It is dangerous, however, if any proposed definition becomes the basis for marginalizing and representing some communities as alien, for hostility, and for mistrust about national loyalties. Although Savarkar includes religion as one dimension of his definition of Hindutva, he assumed that Hindu religious traditions would concur with his definition of Hindu identity. He did not consider the possibility that there

may be elements of his definition of the Hindu identity inconsistent with the core theological claims of the Hindu tradition.
On the basis of these claims, Savarkar's Hindutva must be challenged and contested. It is to these challenges that I now turn.

Nationalism and Idolatry

First, Hindutva is a philosophy of religious nationalism that
divinizes the land of India and proposes the highest aim of life
to be the service and defense of the motherland. Although the
Hindu tradition affirms the immanence of the divine and invites
us to see the divine in the natural world, it does not limit this
geographically and speaks of an ultimate divine transcendence.

The Kena Upaniṣad, which belongs to the Sāma Veda, cautions us in a series of verses (1:4–8) about the dangers of mis-
taking the finite for the infinite and of worshipping the finite.[12]
In a series of five verses, the teacher differentiates the finite
from the infinite. In each verse, he instructs that the infinite is
not a worldly object, not even one that can be worshipped by
people. It is a classic criticism of idolatry, understood here as
the error of substituting that which is finite for the infinite. The
Kena Upaniṣad regards such idolatry as having its roots in ignorance (*avidyā*) about the nature of the infinite *brahman*. The
Kena Upaniṣad does not specifically mention the nation, but
when the finite nation becomes an object of ultimate value and
worship, the dangers of ignorance (*avidyā*) and idolatry multi-
ply. Invoking the nation as an object of ultimate value too often
means that actions undertaken in the name of the nation are
exempt from criticism and that criticism is regarded as sacrile-
gious and as a treacherous act of disloyalty.

The glorification of the nation is often, in actuality, the
exaltation of a particular ethnic or religious community above
other groups that are considered to have lesser worth. The spiritual obstacles of egocentrism, however, highlighted in the

Hindu tradition, do not disappear when these are projected and transferred onto the nation and when we exalt ourselves in the name of our nations. In fact, these become even more dangerous when professed in the name of the nation, since there is a self-deception and an absence of self-criticism that conceals the betrayal of religious values.

The problems of attributing ultimate value to a finite nation take a sinister turn, with violent consequences, when definitions of the nation and national identity, like the one proffered by Savarkar, are championed to exclude some communities and to privilege others. Savarkar's definition of *Hinduness* and its adoption by Hindu nationalists is associated with attitudes of hostility, mistrust, and increasing violence toward Christian and Muslim minority communities that do not satisfy his criteria. It is an example of holding the nation and a version of national identity as an ultimate value. Hindutva does not offer us any transcendent source of meaning from which one may interrogate the idea of the nation and constructions of national identity. Theologically, Hindutva pantheistically identifies the divine with the land of India and, in doing so, overlooks and negates divine transcendence, which is so important in the teachings of the Upaniṣads.

It is not realistic to expect the dissolution of national walls, but the Hindu tradition requires that we profess our national identities lightly, never losing sight of the more fundamental truth of a universe and living beings united by having their origin in a single divine source, described in the Taittirīya Upaniṣad (3.1.1) as "that from which all beings originate, by which they are sustained and to which they return." Theologically, there is a great emphasis on our shared identity with all beings originating from the teaching that the infinite *brahman* exists identically in all beings. The tradition invites us to see ourselves in everyone. Hindutva does not value this universal shared identity and is founded on differences between Hindus and non-Hindus. Any version of nationalism and national identity that undermines the dignity of others or that justifies and instigates violence is contrary to the fundamental teachings of the Hindu tradition. Hindu-Christian dialogue requires openness to the fact that divinization of a nation is not the only way that religious communities express national commitments. Divinization of the nation must not become a test of nationalism.

Religious Identity and National Identity

Hindu nationalism conflates religious and national identity. For Savarkar, *Hindu* is both a religious and a national identity. The national loyalty of Indian Christians and Muslims, followers of "alien" religions, is regarded with suspicion. In Savarkar's view, the Hindu religious tradition does not make universal theological claims but addresses itself only to a specific national, ethnic, and cultural community. Hindutva overlooks the universalism of Hinduism and narrowly identifies it with the nation and common ancestry (*jāti*). Savarkar demonstrates no interest in the truth or untruth of religious claims. Religion is instrumentalized as a component of national identity.

Dialogue is impossible when religious truths are reduced to ethnocentric truths. Savarkar's version of Hinduism offers no justification or reason for dialogue with Christians or any other tradition. It does not surprise anyone, therefore, that Hindu nationalists exemplify no interest in Hindu-Christian dialogue.

The disservice that Hindu nationalism does to the Hindu religious tradition could be illustrated by comparing Savarkar's Hindu nationalism with that of Swami Vivekananda (1863–1902), who represented Hinduism at the Parliament of the World's Religions held in Chicago in 1893 and who, in 1895, founded both the Vedānta Society in New York and the Ramakrishna Mission in India. Vivekananda used the terms *Hindu* and *Hinduism* to denote a religious identity and, most importantly, did not distinguish, like Savarkar, between *Hindu* and *Hinduism*. This distinction, to remind ourselves, was central to Savarkar's discussion. For Savarkar, *Hinduism* is only the "ism" of the Hindu and refers specifically to the system of religious belief and practice. *Hindu*, on the other hand, refers to the territorial, ethnic, and cultural factors constituting the Hindu nation. One cannot, for Savarkar, determine the character of Hinduism without first defining who is a Hindu.

For Vivekananda, a Hindu, first and foremost, is a person who subscribes to the religious worldview of Hinduism. In Swami Vivekananda's first major address before the Parliament of Religions, delivered on September 19, 1893, he consistently used the word *Hindu* as being indicative of religious belief.[13] In one of his most important addresses entitled "The Common Basis of Hinduism" and delivered in the city of Lahore after his return to India from the Parliament of Religions, Swami Vivekananda identified the doctrines shared by all Hindus.[14] A Hindu, according to Vivekananda, is one who believes in the following: the authority of the Vedas; God; the cyclical order of creation, preservation, and dissolution; the immortality of the true self and its innate purity and perfection; and reincarnation and religion as realization. Such teachings are universal and open to any human being.

The land of India has special sacred significance for Vivekananda, and like Savarkar, he refers to India as a *puṇyabhumi*. He uses the term, however, in a descriptive and not prescriptive manner to express his veneration for India as a land of spirituality and as the place of origin for several of the world's religions. There is no evidence in Vivekananda's lectures and writings to suggest that he uses the term like Savarkar, as a fundamental requirement of Hindu identity and as a criterion of demarcation and exclusion of Christians and Muslims.[15] As Ainslie T. Embree notes, Vivekananda's love for India and

Hinduism was never exclusive, and "above all it was never anti-Muslim or anti-Christian."[16]

Although he was a passionate nationalist and great lover of India and her people, Swami Vivekananda treated Hinduism as a distinctive worldview with a relevance and appeal that transcends ties of nationality, ethnicity, and culture. In his lectures to western audiences, he presented the Hindu tradition as one that universally addresses the human condition and predicament and as a real option for people who do not have ancestral or cultural roots in the Indian subcontinent. He was the earliest to envisage and articulate that possibility. We may say that being Hindu for Swami Vivekananda was not the same as being Indian. For Hindu nationalists, these are one and the same.

The Devalued Other

Hindutva makes a sharp distinction between Hindus and non-Hindus. It thrives upon this distinction and a devalued other. Hinduism, on the other hand, calls attention to unity of all existence in the infinite *brahman* and to the necessity of being committed to the well-being of all. The inherent worth of the individual human person proceeds from the belief that each one embodies this infinite one. The various traditions of Hinduism have characterized the relationship between the divine spirit and the human self in various ways, dependent on their philosophical standpoints. The nondualists speak of the identity of the two while the qualified nondualists describe the relationship as one of inseparability but not identity. All of them agree, however, on the fact that the divine exists equally and identically in all beings. As the Bhagavadgītā (13:27) puts it,

> One who sees the supreme Lord,
> Existing alike in all beings,

> Not perishing when they perish,
> Truly sees.[17]

While the social and political implications of this truth are not detailed in the classical texts, the consequences are unmistakable. When the implications for human relationships are enunciated, these are done in terms of equality. As the Bhagavadgītā (5:19) states,

> Even here on earth, those whose minds are impartial
>   overcome rebirth. God
> is perfect and the same in all. Therefore, they always
>   abide in God.[18]

Justice, understood as equality of treatment, is a consequence of the equal presence of the divine.

The Hindu teaching of the unity of existence through the divine and in the sacredness of all life that expresses the divine is the foundation of its cardinal ethical principle, *ahiṃsā* (non-injury). Belief in divine immanence requires the demonstration of reverence and consideration for life in all its forms and the avoidance of injury. In his understanding and interpretation of the meaning of *ahiṃsā*, Gandhi explained that in its negative form, it means abstention from injury to living beings. In its positive form, *ahiṃsā* means love and compassion for all. For Gandhi, *ahiṃsā* also implies justice toward everyone and abstention from exploitation in any form. "No man," claimed Gandhi, "could be actively non-violent and not rise against social injustice no matter where it occurred."[19]

The implication of teachings like these is that Hindus must affirm the dignity and equal worth of all human beings. This is our spiritual antidote to any effort to deny the personhood of others. We cannot honor and value the divine and devalue human beings. We cannot give our assent or support to any social or cultural system that is founded on human inequality and indignity. Our understanding of God requires diligence and discernment in identifying such systems and in articulating critiques from our theological centers. To ascribe unequal worth to persons on the basis of religious identity and to deprive them of equal rights in the civic sphere contradicts the fundamental teachings and values of the Hindu tradition. This criticism applies equally to the hierarchical ordering of Hindu society into castes with unequal rights and privileges. We must not make hostility to Christians and Muslims a requirement of commitment to Hinduism or Hindu identity.

Celebrating Diversity

Hindutva champions a form of majority rule that appears to be intolerant of plural identities by asserting a definition of nationality and loyalty that excludes large numbers of people for whom India is home. Such definitions also raise crucial questions about the nature of Hinduism as a world religion and its role in world affairs.

There is an ancient and powerful tradition of hospitality to religious diversity in the Hindu tradition that made it possible to accommodate a wide diversity of religious beliefs and practices and to offer shelter to persecuted religious groups for centuries. It is this genuine hospitality that can once again point the way forward as India agonizes over its identity as a nation. While no political system can afford to ignore the concerns of its majority community, if India opts for a form of majority rule that is intolerant of plural identities, it would send a tragic message to other countries that are struggling with the challenges of diversity and seeking to find ways of building cohesive communities within their diversity. I wish that more Hindu leaders in India and in other parts of the world could see how detrimental Savarkar's definition of Hinduism is for the tradition and its potential to benefit our world. India has the resources in its traditions for constructing a national identity out of the wealth of its diversity, but it needs to reject and look beyond the definition championed by Savarkar. This may yet be one of its greatest contribution to world affairs.

A robust Hindu theology of religious diversity could counter the tendency and temptation on the part of religious nationalists to see the state as an instrument for enforcing a particular religious doctrine. By detaching themselves from Hindutva, Hindu religious traditions can again become eloquent champions of a pluralism that allows different groups the freedom of self-definition, that promotes dialogue and cooperation, and that engages all in a search for a national identity that reflects the wealth of India's diversity.

It is beyond the scope of this book to discuss the complexities of Hindu approaches to diversity; here I identity only a few salient features. As a consequence of the antiquity and interaction among India's diverse religious and cultural traditions, Hinduism has developed approaches and insights that are essentially pluralistic in nature and that complement and are congenial to a value for pluralism in the political sphere.[20] The different Hindu philosophical systems are referred to as *darśanas* (lit. "ways of seeing"). These different ways of seeing express our temporal, spatial, and cultural locations as well as our identities, individually and as members of groups. Plurality, in other words, is a natural outcome of human diversity. The divine is always more than we can define, describe, or understand with our finite minds, and descriptions will, of necessity, be plural. The acknowledgment of the limits of language and the relativity of the human condition preclude any Hindu claim to the ownership of truth in its fullness and finality. Hinduism espouses an epistemological and philosophical humility that is antithetical to the privileging of a single viewpoint, religious or political, and recognizes the enrichment that diversity affords.

The desire for religious or political hegemony and homogeneity is not in accord with the foundations of the Hindu worldview. Along with arguments for plurality rooted in the diversity of human nature and locations, Hindu traditions have also called attention to the limits of human language and symbols.

Conclusion

> So foreign races in Hindusthan must either adopt the Hindu culture and language, must learn to respect and hold in reverence the Hindu religion, must entertain no idea but those of the glorification of the Hindu race and culture, i.e., of the Hindu nation and must lose their separate existence to merge in the Hindu race, or may stay in the country, wholly subordinated to the Hindu Nation, claiming nothing, deserving no privileges, far less any preferential treatment—not even citizen's rights.[21]

The words above are from Madhav Sadashiv Golwalkar (1906–73), who was the successor to Hedgewar as leader of the Rashtriya Swayamsevak Sangh (RSS). Perhaps the implication of these words may be better appreciated if we substituted "Europe" or "America" for Hindustan. Today, Hindus live as minorities in many parts of the world. They desire to participate fully in the lives of their new homelands while, at the same time, preserving a distinctive identity as followers of Hinduism. Most of them still regard India as a spiritual homeland (*punyabhumi*). They would shudder at any definition of national identity that required them to relinquish their historical identities as the price of acceptance and participation.

Hindu Americans know well the fears and the challenges of being a religious minority. They have participated in many legal and lobbying efforts to ensure that federal, state, and city policies are not partial to the interests of the religious majority or a single tradition. They affirm the right to self-definition and resist coercion to have the religious beliefs of others imposed on them. They contest monolithic definitions of American identity that would marginalize and exclude them. The continuing growth of Hindu and other Asian traditions on American soil is made possible by the framework of America's pluralistic democracy and the constitutional provision that the state does not regulate or enforce religion or use religion as a basis for unequal privileges. This argument does not suggest that the particular religions do not enjoy privilege on American soil, but constitutional guarantees provide a remedy for the ongoing challenge to such privileges.[22]

Although the challenge of being a religious minority is new for most Hindu Americans, the experience is also an opportunity for understanding the predicament of religious minorities in India and other parts of our world. As Hindus, we must lift our voices in concern against ideologies that are intolerant of plural religious identities or make demands that violate religious freedom. We can and must affirm a Hindu tradition that is not narrowly identified with a particular nation but speaks to human beings across the boundaries of nationality, race, and ethnicity and advocates for democratic pluralism across our world.

There are always grave dangers when religion and nation are identified. One such danger is that the entire meaning, purpose, and potential of a religion is narrowly interpreted through the lens of national political interests at any given moment in time. Religious traditions surrender their moral power to the state and become subservient to its narrow agenda. This is a dangerous religious malfunction. In situations of political rivalry and hostility, like that obtaining between India and Pakistan, where the majority in each nation identifies with a different religion, the result is that the meaning of one's religious identity comes to include hate and hostility for those belonging to the other tradition. This virus of hate spreads rapidly and distorts religious commitments. Freedom from hate requires that we see our traditions, not as being national or ethnic religions, but as making universal claims about what is true, good, and beautiful and as affirming dignity for all beings. The challenge of reclaiming our traditions from those who narrowly identify it with nation and who believe that it legitimizes hate for religious others is urgent and must not be underestimated.

Most importantly, interreligious dialogue becomes impossible if we profess definitions of national identity that delegitimize the commitments of our religious partners and deny them opportunities for equal participation in national life.

CHAPTER FOUR

Caste and Hindu-Christian Dialogue

The overwhelming majority of Christians in India come from the Dalit communities, members of the so-called untouchable groups. Most converted in the hope of escaping oppression under the caste system and their impoverished living conditions. The Indian census (2011) puts the Indian Christian population at 2.3 percent of the total population.[1] It is estimated that between 50 percent and 75 percent of Indian Christians are Dalit converts, even though the figures are unreliable, since the category is not an official one.[2] The situation does not seem to be very different for Indian Muslims. Over 75 percent of the present Indian Muslim population is of Dalit origin.[3]

In 1956, almost half a million Dalits converted to Buddhism, responding to the call of B. R. Ambedkar to reject the caste system.[4] In 1935, Ambedkar made a powerful declaration of his intent in these famous words: "Unfortunately, I was born a Hindu Untouchable. It was beyond my power to prevent that. But it is within my power to refuse to live within these humiliating conditions. Though I was born a Hindu, I solemnly assure you that I will not die as a Hindu."[5]

In 1935, Ambedkar listed a number of sharp and powerful questions that so-called untouchables must address to the Hindu tradition. These questions are as valid today as they were eight decades ago:

Does Hinduism recognize their worth as human beings? Does it stand for their equality? Does it extend to them the benefit of liberty? Does it at least help to forge the bond of fraternity between them and the Hindus? Does it teach the Hindus that the Untouchables are their kindred? Does it say to the Hindus it is a sin to treat the Untouchables as being neither man nor beast? Does it tell the Hindus to be righteous to the Untouchables? Does it preach to the Hindus to be just and humane to them? Does it inculcate upon the Hindus the virtue of being friendly to them? Does it tell Hindus to love them, to respect them and to do them no wrong? In fine, does Hinduism universalize the value of life without distinction?[6]

The Challenges of Caste for Hinduism

Hindus continue to express concerns about conversion to other religions, and as noted earlier, several Indian states have enacted legislation to prohibit conversions through coercion, allurement, and fraud. There are also calls for national anticonversion laws. What continues to be missing from the Hindu side are serious efforts to understand the attractiveness of Christianity and other religions to the convert. It must be instructive and challenging for Hindus that the largest numbers of converts to Christianity come from the so-called untouchable castes. It should be obvious that people from the untouchable castes experience the tradition as oppressive and as negating their dignity and self-worth. For such persons, the Christian message of the inclusive love of God and acceptance in a community where human equality and value are affirmed is attractive and liberative. In the words of Ambedkar, conversion offered the untouchables the "opportunity to be members of a community whose religion has universalized and equalized all values in life."[7]

As an alternative to serious engagement with the oppressive structures of caste, we choose to be accusatory. We characterize the convert as a childlike and immature individual who is incapable of exercising choice and judgment and who does not know what is good for her. We treat the convert as ignorant and simpleminded, subject to easy manipulation and deceit. We prefer to think that the convert does not cross religious boundaries because of any legitimate dissatisfaction with inherited tradition or anything of intrinsic worth in the other tradition. It is less challenging for us to think of conversion as the consequence of coercion or material inducement and not as suggesting something problematic in our tradition or theologically attractive in the other.

At a fundamental level, the convert disturbs and unsettles us, and our discomfort finds expression in antipathy. The act of embracing a different religious tradition sharply challenges our settled assumptions about the adequacy of our religious worldview. Conversion disturbs us by holding out the possibility that our answers are not the only ones or the only satisfactory ones. We see the act of conversion as one of primal rejection and, because our traditions so deeply define our identities, as one of disloyalty to us and to our community.

Many of us who are hostile to the convert act as such from positions of power and privilege within our traditions. Since we experience our religious traditions as being good for us, we assume that it is similarly good for all who are born into it. Through circumstances of birth and opportunity, we live in our traditions without ever experiencing oppression and violence that demean and negate our dignity and self-value. We do not see how what may be good for us may not be good for others whose experiences within our faith may be quite different. We do not see and speak of our tradition with the eyes and voices of the marginalized and despised. It is a sad fact that concerns about conversion are among the few occasions when Dalits attract Hindu upper caste attention.

Conversion is a challenge but also an opportunity for Hindu leaders to consider the relationship between religious doctrine and practice and systemic social and economic structures that condemn millions to lives of poverty, indignity, and exclusion from full participation in the tradition. The tradition needs to go beyond regarding the convert as a childlike individual who must be always protected from the lures and deceptive practices of missionaries.

The Nature and Antiquity of Untouchability

Theories abound about the origins of caste. What is uncontested and important for our purposes is that the group identified with the Ṛg Veda thought of and referred to themselves as *āryas* (noble, of noble descent, pure) and defined themselves over and against others who were referred to as *dāsas* or *dāsyus*. The *dāsyus* were considered to be subhuman, hypocritical, and without virtue, observing different customs and likened to a famine.[8]

By around 800 BCE, the Ṛg Veda *āryas* had consolidated themselves in relation to various non-*ārya* groups and systematized their relationship in the form of the hierarchically structured *varṇa*-system. The *brāhmaṇas* (priests) occupied the top, followed by the *kṣatriyas* (soldiers), *vaiśyas* (merchants and farmers), and *śūdras* (laborers). The first three groups are regarded as the *dvijas*, or twice-born, and are entitled to perform and participate in Vedic ritual. Most importantly, male members of these groups alone underwent the initiatory ritual (*upanayana*) that enabled them to study the Vedas. The incorporation of the *śūdras* into the system, along with their servile status, supports the hypothesis that they represent the "others" who were gradually included into the complex social order. It is also possible that a policy of appeasement was practiced that rewarded cooperative non-*āryas* with elevation to membership in the upper *varṇas.*[9]

Not all non-*ārya* groups, however, were assimilated and incorporated. It is likely that some groups resisted or were not offered the "privilege" of becoming part of the *ārya* hierarchy. Such "hostile" groups, such as the *cāṇḍālas* and *śvapacas*, were declared ritually impure and segregated. The *cāṇḍālas*, for example, were equated with animals and considered unfit even to eat the remnants of another's meals. By the time of Manu (ca. 150 BCE), it was believed that birth into a particular caste was the consequence of karma, or the maturation of past moral actions in the present life. For bad deeds in this life, one could be reborn as a dog, a boar, or a *cāṇḍāla*, in this order. From its early use to refer to a specific group, *cāṇḍāla* became a general term for the untouchable other.

Numerous injunctions based on general features of the *varṇa* system such as the polarity of purity and impurity, hereditary occupations, and the idea of the *dvija* (twice-born) led to the institution of innumerable injunctions against those groups now branded as *aspṛśya* (lit. "untouchable"). By the period between 400 BCE and 400 CE, standard features of untouchability such as physical segregation, noncommensality, and nonconnubiality are firmly in place. The Vedas are not to be studied in a village where *cāṇḍālas* reside. Food offered in ritual is defiled if seen by a *cāṇḍāla*, and sacrificial vessels are rendered impure by their touch. The texts specifying prohibitions against the *cāṇḍālas* group them with animals. Food and ritual vessels are polluted also if seen and touched by dogs, crows, or donkeys. Based on the most recent Indian census (2011), members of the Scheduled Castes and Scheduled Tribes constitute 25 percent of India's population.[10] The Scheduled Castes alone number over two hundred million.

Caste is a hierarchical or graded ordering of human beings based on notions of purity and impurity. Those in the upper echelons of the caste order are ascribed greater purity. Those outside the fourfold order are impure and capable of polluting others by contact. Hence, they are regarded as untouchable (*aspṛśya*). A person's place on the order is determined by birth, and thus caste, like race, is inherited.[11]

Rules and rituals evolved to prohibit and limit relationships and contact between pure and impure groups. These include commensality or eating restrictions. Generally, food may be accepted from and shared with members of one's caste or a higher caste. Contact was also controlled by endogamy restrictions that limited marriage to partners within a caste and by physical segregation in local communities. Most importantly, membership in a particular caste is determined by birth. One is born into a caste, even as one is born into a so-called race. Although there is change in the contemporary Hindu world with access to education and economic opportunities, birth still significantly determines occupation and thus defines and limits one's human possibilities. Since caste is a social ordering based not on wealth but on notions of purity and impurity, professional or economic success does not alter easily one's standing in the hierarchy.

The doctrine of karma was rigidly interpreted to explain all events in the present life, including one's status in the caste system, as having causes that may be traced to actions performed earlier in this life or previous lives. Escape from birth in a lower caste is possible only by rebirth into a higher caste. In such a rigid interpretation of karma, there is no injustice in the social order. Suffering is justified as the consequence of past life actions. The writer D. C. Sharma, for example, attributes social inequalities to karma: "On no other hypothesis, can we explain the inequalities of life that we see all around us. God is not partial. He would not of his own accord make one man strong and another weak, one man healthy and another man sickly, and one man sensual and another man spiritual. He would never of his own accord put one man in surroundings that help the progress of his soul and another man in surroundings that hinder his progress. The inequalities of life are due to us and not to God. We carry our own past."[12]

Vivekanand Jha describes caste as intrinsically exploitative: "There are crude statements to the effect that the *vaisya* and *sudra* are to be exploited for the advantage of the ruling class with the brahmana's active cooperation and help. The Aitareya Brahmana characterizes a *vaisya* as *anyasya balikrit*, 'tributary to another,' *anyasyadya*, 'to be eaten or lived upon by another,' and *yathakamajyeya*, 'to be oppressed at will,' and a *sudra* as *anyasya presya*, 'to be expelled at will,' and *yathakamavadhya*, 'to be slain at will.'"[13]

Exploitation of labor and limited access to material resources were greater as one went down in the caste hierarchy. Purity and impurity distinctions were employed to assign places in the social order, create boundaries, and exploit. The legacy of unequal access to and distribution of material resources continues. One recent study shows that despite a general improvement in income levels among all Indians, poverty is still highly concentrated among traditionally disadvantaged groups such as the Dalits and Adivasis.[14]

Caste identity "continues to define opportunities available to individuals. Landownership patterns remain unequal; lower castes have low educational status; have lower consumption expenditure resulting in lower access to nutrition, healthcare and private education; and have fewer social connections to seek help in emergencies or to provide access to information and connections to important social institutions such as government services, healthcare and medical services. This unequal opportunity and access may well be the root cause of observed inequalities in health outcomes as well as other aspects of well-being."[15]

Caste and Conversion

Hindu activists and commentators see conversion as the consequence of an obsession in the Christian tradition and its aggressive methods. After failing to convert Brahmins, according to the Hindu leader Ashok Chowgule, the church turned its attention to members of the lower caste. Chowgule denies the agency of the lower castes and sees conversion entirely as the outcome of the power of the missionary and his material inducements: "Only when they could not make a dent with the Brahmins that the missionaries turned to the lower castes. The conversions were obtained through inducements and not through any spiritual conviction. They were somewhat successful only when temporal power was with the invading Christians and the area was effectively a colony. The missionaries could project themselves to be benefactors of the lower castes and ensure that governmental largesse would flow to them."[16]

The late Swami Dayananda Saraswati, prominent Hindu teacher and leader, described conversion as an act of violence and not as a quest for freedom from the violence of caste oppression. In the words of Swami Dayananda,

> Religious conversion by missionary activity remains an act of violence. It is an act of violence because it hurts deeply, not only the other members of the family of the converted, but the entire community that comes to know of it. One is connected to various persons in one's world. The religious person in every individual is the innermost, inasmuch as he or she is connected to a force beyond the empirical. The religious person is connected only to the force beyond he has now accepted. That is the reason why the hurt caused by religion can turn into violence. That is why a religious belief can motivate a missionary to be a martyr. When the hurt of the

religious becomes acute, it explodes into violence. Conversion is violence. It generates violence.[17]

Dalit theologian Sathianathan Clarke, on the other hand, describes conversion as a comprehensive rejection of and freedom from Hindu oppressive structures: "Religious conversion for Dalits thus includes a form of boundary smashing and boundary shaping that involves drastic erasure and thorough replacement of inherited but detrimental Word-visions and world-ways. It represents a decision away from intra-house options of minimalist tinkering with elements or maximalist transformations with structures of the Hindu vision and way. Rather conversion represents a vociferous NO to the entire religious, social, political and cultural system."[18]

Dalit Christians see conversion as offering freedom from the oppression of caste and providing a way to cross over into a new religious community that affirms social dignity and worth. Thomas Thangaraj, a Christian theologian, details the story of a group in the southern part of Tamil Nadu from a village named Chanpattu who converted to Christianity in 1804 and renamed their village Nazareth.[19] Members were Nadars, a lower caste community. As a low caste group, the Nadars were not allowed to read Hindu scriptures. Conversion to Christianity was a dramatic turnaround for this group. They changed the name of their village and adopted biblical and Western names. Debarred from reading the Vedas, Nazareth Christians received the Bible with great joy. They displayed great pride in having personal copies of the Bible and spoke of it as Vedam. In this way, they considered themselves to be possessors of the Veda, a text they were debarred from reading. For the first time, they joined a voluntary association that they owned, and they were in control of its affairs. They were empowered by the fact that they built, owned, and used their own place of worship.

The descendants of the Nazareth Christians continue to have a negative view of the Hindu tradition, seeking to emphasize differences with their Hindu neighbors and affirm their distinctive Christian identity. For the Nazareth Christians, conversion to Christianity was an unprecedented opportunity for liberation and religious self-determination. Dalit Christians see their conversion to Christianity as an escape from the violence of caste, psychologically and physically. In the words of Clarke, they embraced "another religious and social framework that valued their own body in relationship to the rest of human society. Body crossings for Dalits was a search for religion to indeed function as a way of life, one that honors their own individual bodies but also gives them a new relationship model for a more elastic social body politic."[20]

Dialogue on Caste and Conversion

Dialogue on conversion between Hindus and Dalit Christians in India is difficult and challenging. This is one of the reasons such dialogue is not occurring in any sustained and meaningful ways. If reconciliation, justice, truth, and peace are important concerns of religion and religious communities, then such dialogue is imperative and must be actively sought.

I think that the Hindu majority community should take the initiative for this dialogue. Religious traditions need to be especially attentive to the voices of those who experience the tradition as oppressive and unjust and as denying them power and freedom. Causing suffering to others (*hiṃsā*) and being indifferent to such suffering are the antithesis of what the Hindu tradition advocates at its highest ethical ideal of nonviolence (*ahiṃsā*). Dalit Christians, who feel alienated from the tradition and who think that the tradition does not accord them dignity and equality, are very unlikely to be the initiators of this dialogue. For them, the value of such a dialogue is questionable.

As noted above, there are radically divergent memories and narratives about conversion in both communities. The outcome of such different narratives is a deep mistrust. Dalit Christians, who see and experience the tradition through the eyes of the oppressed, think that Hindu concerns about conversion are disguised efforts to preserve the privileges and power relationships inherent in the hierarchy of caste. Hindus, on the other hand, treat the convert as a childlike individual lured away from community by the seductive and unethical promises of Christian missionaries. They see the convert as someone who needs to be protected. There is a widespread Hindu suspicion of Christianity as a tradition that is concerned only with increasing its power through conversion and even suspicions about long-term political goals.

In these circumstances of suspicion about motives, trust is a necessity for dialogue. Such trust will not be easy or immediate, and Hindu religious leaders have a special responsibility for nurturing its birth and growth. Trust is the source of hope that narratives and experiences could be shared and that each community could be mindfully attentive to the voices of the other. Trust allows painful stories to be shared and difficult questions to be asked. Trust enables identification with the others' suffering and makes possible self-criticism and transformation. The building of such trust is not a single event but the nurturing of a relationship that cannot be rushed.

Our hope is that in the trustful sharing of experiences, truth will emerge. Interreligious dialogue cannot be indifferent to truth. Hindus must be willing to receive Dalit truths, however difficult and challenging. Hindus will be challenged by Dalit Christians to understand the many ways in which they experience the tradition as oppressive and as negating their human dignity and self-worth. Most Hindu leaders come from males of the upper castes who have always experienced power and privilege within the tradition. Having never experienced religiously justified oppression and injustice, they may assume that the tradition that has been good to them is good for all born within it. Dialogue is an opportunity for Dalits to ask questions about caste and an opportunity for Hindus to speak about those teachings in their tradition that affirm the equal worth and dignity of all human beings and to explain failures, past and present, to implement such teachings in actual life.

The speaking of truth in this dialogue does not aim for consensus. The success of interreligious dialogue is not to be judged only by agreement. It affords a space for sharing and questioning that will hopefully lead to mutual respect, understanding, and the experience of our shared humanity. Dalits must be allowed to articulate the reasons for their embrace of another tradition; the integrity of such a choice and identity must be respected and be the basis for meaningful relationships with Hindus.

The aim of this dialogue is not also reclaiming Dalit Christians as Hindus. The question of whether the Dalits are Hindus or not sharply divided the approaches of the Dalit leader B. R. Ambedkar from those of Mahatma Gandhi. Gandhi believed that the untouchables belonged to the Hindu fold and that untouchability was an aberration that must be expunged. He argued, however, for the retention of the four *varnas* and the performance of hereditary occupations. Ambedkar, on the other hand, argued that untouchables were not Hindus, since they were not included in the *varna* system. We must be especially attentive to Dalit voices who question and are deeply suspicious of what they see as Hindu efforts to define their identity. In this regard, the words of Kancha Ilaiah, Dalit activist and writer, are important:

> I was not born a Hindu for the simple reason that my parents did not know that they were Hindus. This does not mean that I was born a Muslim, a Christian, a Buddhist, a Sikh or a Parsee. My illiterate parents, who lived

in a remote South Indian village, did not know that they belonged to any religion at all. People belong to a religion only when they know that they are a part of the people who worship that God, when they go to those temples and take part in the rituals and festivals of that religion. My parents had only one identity and that was their caste: they were Kurumaas.[21]

Dalits issue an important challenge to those who claim them as Hindus to tell them which morality is Hindu morality. Ilaiah's questions are penetrating and cannot be ignored by Hindus. "Which values," he asks, "do they want to uphold as right values? The 'upper' caste Hindu unequal and inhuman cultural values or our cultural values? What is the ideal of society today? What shall we teach the children of today? Shall we teach them what has been taught by the Hindus or what the dalitbahujan masses of this country want to learn?"[22]

The primary challenge for Hindus is not claiming Dalits as Hindus but owning the more demanding responsibility for the historical, physical, and psychological brutalization of the Dalits by representing them as the untouchable other in relation to those whose Hindu identity is affirmed. It is the task of identifying and repudiating doctrines and customs that profess the unequal worth of others and legitimize their dehumanization and humiliation. It is the task of moving from defensive apologetic to self-criticism and articulating a vision of the tradition that affirms human dignity and worth. It is responding to Ilaiah's challenge by defining clearly the core values of the tradition, especially in relation to systems like caste. Defensive arguments that suggest a harmonious and noble original intention underlying caste do nothing to define these values or deal with the reality of oppression.

Confronting Together and Overcoming Caste

There are many Christians who see the Hindu concern with conversion as a disguised effort to preserve the privileges and power relationships inherent in the caste system. We cannot ignore, however, the fact that even the Christian church in India has not been able to free itself from the social inequities and expressions of caste.

Dalit Catholics, for example constitute 65 percent of the total population of Indian Catholics and are grossly under-represented in official church positions. In the words of Joe Jose, "Dalit Christians are forced to live with the dual identity of being a Dalit first and a converted Dalit Christian later. Unfortunately, even if Dalit converts refuse to identify themselves with their caste, their identity is often reflected in their socio-cultural life, as they are viewed as Dalits even after a change in their faith."[23] In the town of Trichy in the state of Tamil Nadu, upper and lower caste Christians are buried on separate sides of a wall. Intercaste marriages among converted Christians are rare.[24] Caste is in evidence in the formation of parishes and in the construction of separate chapels in villages for Dalits and other Christians.[25]

The existence of caste across religious communities is no comfort to those who are crushed by its oppressive weight, and it is not an argument that should be made by Hindus to defend or excuse caste. Ambedkar, for example, does not question the reality of caste in other communities but highlights critical differences. The most significant among these is that other traditions have not treated caste as a sacred order legitimized by religion. For Ambedkar, "it is, therefore, a dangerous delusion to take comfort in the mere existence of caste among non-Hindus, without caring to know what place caste occupies in their life and whether there are other 'organic filaments' which subordinate the feelings of caste to the feelings of community. The sooner the Hindus are cured of this delusion, the better."[26]

At the same time, the persistence of caste in other communities, even after conversion, points to it having a transreligious nature. Caste, like race, is one historical example of a hierarchical ordering of human beings based on notions of superiority and inferiority and unequal access to material and social resources. I believe that there are theological visions at the heart of both Hinduism and Christianity that invalidate the assumptions of inequality, powerlessness, impurity, and indignity that are at the foundations of caste belief and practice. This must be recognized and affirmed by both traditions and become the basis of mutual support and cooperation for the overcoming of oppressive systems of human hierarchy and the promotion of human flourishing.[27]

We can stand together and join our voices against any ideology, as well as political or social structures, that denies the personhood and dignity of human beings and that condones injustice and irreverence. We can speak together for justice and do so for reasons that include but go beyond the political and economic; we can speak of the divine presence at the heart of the human.

Conclusion

Hindus have an important obligation to acknowledge the inhumanity, injustice, and oppression of the caste system and the fact that it has been legitimized and perpetuated by appeal to and interpretations of Hindu teachings. It is still understood by too many Hindus as a mark of their religious identity and has a pervasive presence in Hindu teaching and practice.

To be meaningful, such an acknowledgment has to be made to the victims of caste violence, with a request for forgiveness (*kṣamā*). It must be accompanied by an unequivocal repudiation of caste as fundamentally incompatible with certain core teachings of the tradition and a commitment to work for its elimination in religious teaching, practice, and daily life. It requires a commitment to support policies that transform historical structures of injustice and that make for more equitable access to resources necessary for human flourishing.

Asking for forgiveness in this way can be more challenging than extending forgiveness, since it requires us to be humbly self-critical and to see clearly our own susceptibility to corruption and our tendency to affirm self-value by devaluing and demeaning others. It prompts us to see how we benefit from a system that is violent in the suffering it inflicts upon others. The training and education of Hindu leaders of every kind must include education about caste injustice, its incompatibility with Hindu teaching, and the nurturing of a commitment to its eradication. A tradition that calls us to see God in all cannot be indifferent to this blatant blindness.

Several years ago, I contributed to the drafting of "A Hindu Apology for Caste and Untouchability," published by Sadhana. I conclude by citing an excerpt from this statement:

> We offer this apology for the suffering that we inflict, cognizant of the work that still lies ahead to overcome caste injustices. Caste assumptions and practices are pervasive and are conveyed through religious ritual, teachings and social norms and practices. We have an urgent responsibility to identify, challenge and transform all such expressions of caste that are oppressive and dehumanizing. We must lift our voices in protest against all practices in the name of our tradition that denigrate other human beings. We must ensure that Hindu leaders take a clear and forceful stand on this matter and repudiate injustice in the name of the Hindu tradition.[28]

CHAPTER FIVE

What Can Hindus Learn from Christianity?

The Christian tradition has been an early and constant presence in my life. This presence took a formal expression later in the mode of interreligious dialogue, but it was there in childhood friendships in a multireligious village on the island of Trinidad where I was born, in the Sunday school classes that we occasionally visited for the stories and treats, in a high school that I attended, which was founded by Canadian Christian Presbyterian missionaries, in public festivals at Easter and Christmas, and for the past three decades, in work at Saint Olaf College, a Lutheran Christian institution of higher education.[1]

Since 1981, my engagement in interreligious dialogue has focused in a special way on Hindu-Christian dialogue. I have had the privilege of being in a continuing relationship with the World Council of Churches, the world's broadest Christian ecumenical body, and the Pontifical Council for Interreligious Dialogue at the Vatican. As part of this work, I have had the honor of meeting Pope John Paul II, Pope Benedict, and most recently, Pope Francis. The influence of the Christian tradition, like that of a good friend, is both subtle and overt, elusive and unmistakable.

I will approach my topic in a twofold manner. From the earliest historical encounters, Hindus have been learning from Christians and Christianity. I will begin briefly with some of the significant Hindu leaders and teachers who acknowledge learning from the Christian tradition and identify the learning that they describe. The history of Hindu-Christian engagement on the Indian subcontinent is long and complex, and I must be selective. Secondly, I will describe, in more personal terms, my own journey of learning from the Christian tradition.

Rammohan Roy

It was in the northeastern region of Bengal in the eighteenth and nineteenth centuries, with the nearby port of Kolkata, where the Christian tradition made its greatest early impact in India, coinciding with the establishment of British control in the same area. Rammohan Roy (1772–1833) was the founder of the Brahmo Samaj, a Hindu reform movement, and the first Hindu to undertake a systematic study of Christianity. In 1820, Roy published *The Precepts of Jesus: The Guide to Peace and Happiness*, a collection of what Roy considered to be Jesus's ethical teachings. Roy clarified his intention in words that are often quoted:

> I feel persuaded that by separating from other matters contained in the New Testament, the moral precepts found in that book, these will be more likely to produce the desirable effect of improving the hearts and minds of men of different persuasions and degrees of understanding. . . . This simple code of religion and morality is so admirably calculated to elevate men's ideas to high and liberal notions of God . . . and is also so well fitted to regulate the conduct of the human race in the discharge of their various duties to themselves, and to society, that I cannot but hope the best effects from its promulgation in the present form.[2]

Roy, who was working to reform Hindu society, found support for this work in the ethics of Jesus. Not surprisingly,

Rammohan Roy opened his collection with Matthew 5:7, which includes the Sermon on the Mount. Roy was the first Hindu to make the effort to disconnect Jesus from institutional Christianity, and all the major Hindu figures in the nineteenth and early twentieth centuries followed his lead. Roy believed that the ethical teachings of Jesus offered resources for the reform of Hindu society and that these teachings could be distinguished from the doctrines of the church about Jesus. It is Roy who called Hindu attention to Jesus, who sought to offer an interpretation of Jesus independent of the doctrines of the Christian church, and who opened the doors for other Hindus to contribute to this discussion.

Keshub Chandra Sen

Like Rammohan Roy, Keshub Chandra Sen (1838–84) also assumed a leadership role in the Brahmo Samaj. In a lecture, "Jesus Christ: Europe and Asia," delivered in Calcutta on May 5, 1866, Sen chastised Europeans for what he called their "muscular Christianity," which caused Hindus to identify Christianity with power, privilege, and violence. Sen claimed Jesus as an Asiatic and spoke of the congeniality of the imageries and analogies, the flora and fauna of the four Gospels to people of Asia:

> I rejoice, yea, I am proud that I am an Asiatic. And was not Jesus Christ an Asiatic? Yes and his disciples were Asiatics, and in Asia. When I reflect on this, my love for Jesus becomes a hundredfold intensified; I feel him nearer to my heart, and deeper in my national sympathies. Why should I then feel ashamed to acknowledge that nationality which he acknowledged? Shall I not rather say, he is more congenial and akin to my oriental nature, more agreeable to my Oriental habits of thought and feeling? And is it not true that an Asiatic

can read the imageries and allegories of the Gospel, and its descriptions of natural sceneries, of customs and manners, with greater interest, and a fuller perception of their force and beauty, than Europeans?[3]

Sen gave prominence in his learning to Jesus's teachings about forgiveness and self-sacrifice: "It is these two cardinal principles of Christian ethics—so utterly opposed to the wisdom of the world, and so far exalted above its highest conceptions of rectitude—which require to be impressed upon the European and native races, as upon the proper appreciation of these, I believe, depends the reformation of their character."[4]

Swami Vivekananda

Swami Vivekananda (1863–1902), one of the most influential Hindu teachers in recent times and the first to teach extensively in the West, made a special appeal for attentiveness to the teachings of Jesus. In his introduction to the Bengali translation of *The Imitation of Christ*, a work attributed to the medieval Catholic monk Thomas Kempis (ca. 1380–1471), Vivekananda cautioned his fellow Hindus not to belittle the text because the author is Christian. This medieval Christian work fascinated Vivekananda, and it was the only text, along with the Bhagavadgītā, that he kept with him during his years of traveling around India after the death of his beloved teacher, Sri Ramakrishna.

Vivekananda founded a new monastic order, the Ramakrishna Math, and a new mission, the Ramakrishna Mission, dedicated to renunciation and service. Active service in the world was not a traditional goal of Hindu monasticism. Vivekananda coined the motto *atmano mokshartham jagat hitaya cha* (for one's own salvation and for the welfare of the world) for the Ramakrishna Mission.

On the night when some of the young disciples of Sri Ramakrishna took monastic vows, Narendra, Vivekananda's pre-monastic name, narrated the story of Jesus for inspiration. As described in one account, he told "the story of the Lord Jesus, beginning with the wondrous mystery of his birth through his death on to the resurrection. Through the eloquence of Narendra, the boys were admitted into that apostolic world wherein Paul has preached the gospel of the Arisen Christ and spread Christianity far and wide. Naren made his plea to them to become Christs themselves, to aid in the redemption of the world; to realize God and deny themselves as the Lord Jesus had done. . . . Strangely the monks discovered afterwards that it was Christmas Eve!"[5] At the moment of establishing one of the most important monastic orders of modern Hinduism, the founder turned to the life of Jesus for inspiration, attracted no doubt by the ideals of renunciation and service in the world exemplified in the life of Jesus.

Mahatma Gandhi

Gandhi turned to Jesus throughout his life for inspiration and never hesitated to acknowledge this fact: "Though I cannot claim to be a Christian in the sectarian sense, the example of Jesus' suffering is a factor in the composition of my underlying faith in non-violence, which rules all my actions, worldly and temporal. Jesus lived and died in vain if he did not teach us to regulate the whole of life by the eternal law of Love."[6]

Gandhi's grandson Rajmohan Gandhi described the cross as "a magnet for Gandhi." In working to bring peace between Muslims and Hindus, Gandhi often faced the wrath of his fellow Hindus. The example of Jesus was a source of inspiration as he faced the anger of his own community: "Jesus Christ prayed to God from the Cross to forgive those who had crucified him. It is my constant prayer to God that He may give me the strength to intercede even for my assassin. And it should be your prayer too that your faithful servant may be given that strength to forgive."[7]

Examples like these may be multiplied. It is remarkable that Hindus like Roy, Vivekananda, Gandhi, and others were commending learning from Jesus and his teachings in a historical context where Christianity was virtually inseparable from colonialism and in which missionaries denounced Hinduism as superstitious, idolatrous, and polytheistic. All of the Hindu leaders that I mention here were inspired by and learned from Jesus. They drank deeply from his teachings and his embodiment of the meaning of an awakening to God for our lives in this world and our human relationships.

At the same time, they had considerable difficulty with institutionalized Christianity. A significant part of the problem here is the alliance they experienced between the institution of the church and colonial rule. Many, in fact, used the teachings and example of Jesus to chastise the church and what they saw as the chasm between the ideals of Jesus and Christian practice. They commended and contrasted Jesus's freedom from greed, his nonpossessiveness, and his generous self-giving with the affluence of the church and the materialism of some Christians. Swami Vivekananda implored his Christian audience in the United States to return to Jesus:

> Yours is religion preached in the name of luxury. What
> an irony of fate! Reverse this if you want to live, reverse
> this. It is all hypocrisy that I have heard in this country.
> If this nation is going to live, let it go back to him. You
> cannot serve God and Mammon at the same time. All
> this prosperity, all this from Christ! Christ would have
> denied all such heresies. All prosperity which comes
> with Mammon is transient, is only for a moment. Real
> permanence is in Him. If you can join these two, this

wonderful prosperity with the ideal of Christ, it is well. But if you cannot, better go back to him and give this up. Better be ready to live in rags with Christ than to live in palaces without him.[8]

Vivekananda's words are interesting for many reasons, but not the least for the fact that we find here a great Hindu teacher chastising and commending the teachings of Jesus to his Christian audience. He is asking them not to become Hindus but to become better Christians—to return to the foundational ideals of Jesus. In a similar way, Gandhi's understanding of nonviolence, nurtured by Jain and Hindu sources, was deepened and enriched by his encounter with the teachings of Jesus, especially the Sermon on the Mount, and his reading of Christian writers like Tolstoy. Gandhi then became one of the most important teachers for Dr. Martin Luther King Jr., who made an extraordinary claim about the significance of Gandhi's understanding of Jesus: "Gandhi was probably the first person in history to lift the love ethic of Jesus above mere interaction between individuals to a powerful and effective social force on a large scale. Love for Gandhi was a potent instrument for social and collective transformation."[9]

My Learning from Christianity

I wish to turn now to the second part of my discussion and to reflect on some salient aspects of my own learning from Christians. Although the roots of my own learning from the Christian tradition are much earlier, I will begin with an event in the year 1981, when I was in the first year of my PhD program at the University of Leeds in the United Kingdom. I was invited by the World Council of Churches to attend a Hindu-Christian dialogue meeting on "Religious Resources for a Just Society" in the small North Indian, Himalayan town of Rajpur. Thirty-two participants, from various parts of the world, were brought together for a week of intense and difficult conversations on religion and justice.

Before embarking on graduate studies in the United Kingdom, I had spent three years in a Hindu monastery in India in seminary-type study. We studied Sanskrit, read sacred texts with commentaries, and practiced meditation. While immersed in traditional study and practice, I did not critically question the content of the curricula. The focus was exclusively on self-inquiry (*ātmā vicāra*) and knowledge for the attainment of liberation, referred to in Sanskrit as *mokṣa*. Since liberation is the highest goal of human life, this attention was appropriate. Its absence would be similar to a ministry curriculum in a Christian seminary that did not significantly discuss sin and salvation. The problem, as I saw much clearer later, was the focus on liberation in a manner that excluded everything else and was disconnected with the challenges of life in the world. The core claims of the tradition, in this case the nondual (*Advaita*), were expounded through ancient texts and commentaries with no attempt to connect and explore the significance of these teachings for social realities. Our teachers were not equipped or did not think it important to make these connections.

The monastery was a place of training and preparation for those who would themselves become teachers to Hindu communities across India. Unless they deviated from this mode of traditional learning, they would also fail to connect religious teaching with the conditions of life in those communities. We never discussed or critically interrogated texts and interpretations that justified the oppressive social hierarchies of caste and patriarchy or read any writings from marginalized groups. Our monastic teachers did not build bridges between the wisdom of the tradition and social justice.

The Rajpur meeting was my first intense participation in a discussion exploring the relationship between religion and justice. I was challenged to think self-critically about my tradi-tion, to explore its resources for a just society, and to grapple with interpretations that justify injustice. I had to look at my traditional learning through the lens of justice. Questions raised at this meeting continue to engage me to this day. Some of the questions asked of the Hindu participants included the following:

> How do Hindus see justice in a social order based on
>   human hierarchy?
> If at a social level there is so much difference between
>   brahmin and *śūdra*, what good is it to know that
>   they are one in *ātman*?
> In the operation of the law of *karma*, is there not a
>   danger of determinism?
> How do you relate the renunciation of the world
>   through *sannyasa* to the concrete problems of
>   social justice?[10]

The challenges of Rajpur and my learning from this meet-ing, I must confess, came more from listening to and engage-ment with the Christian participants who exemplified a greater willingness to interrogate religious teachings and practices that perpetuate injustice. Permit me to share my unpublished notes from 1981 on this matter:

> On the subject of religious resources for a just society,
> the trend of Hindu participation, with notable excep-
> tions, was an echo of the British Orientalism of the
> nineteenth century. There was a constant harking back
> to the past and its glorification. . . . We did not seem to
> be addressing the urgent task of critically and creatively
> exploring tradition in the light of present realities, for
> there are undoubtedly vast resources of symbols and
> ideals in the Hindu tradition which can become a fertile

source of inspiration for action directed towards the creation of a just society. . . . It is not enough to proffer Yoga as a panacea for all forms of human injustice . . . without being aware of the highly individualistic basis on which its philosophy and values have been traditionally understood. Certainly, if systems like Yoga are to play any part in combating injustice, their values will have to be radically extended and reinterpreted.

Liberation Theology

Although I cannot recall if the term *liberation theology* was used by Christian participants, I recognized later that a lot of what I heard from them were central elements of this theology. For the liberation theologian, religion and justice are inseparable. The practice of justice in human relationships is a fundamental expression of religious life. The interior religious life must find outward expression in a commitment to justice. These two dimensions mutually nourish and are incomplete without each other. Without the concern for justice, personal piety becomes obsessively self-centered. At the same time, attentiveness to and cultivation of the interior spiritual life nourish and provide the motivation for the work of justice. Justice cannot be equated with charity. Charity seeks to offer relief and care to those who are the victims of injustice. Justice seeks to change and transform the structures that cause suffering. One of the distinguishing marks of liberation theology is that the commitment to economic, political, and social freedom is rooted in a religious worldview in which the understanding of what it means to be human is derived from a vision of the nature of the divine. Compassion and generosity were known to me as core Hindu teachings but were limited to interpersonal relationships. What was new was the call to interrogate and transform structures of injustice that cause suffering by oppression and by limiting access to resources necessary for human well-being.

The necessity to historically connect religious teaching with life in community and to address injustice and oppression within my tradition have engaged my work as a Hindu scholar and practitioner. Since Rajpur, I have participated in numerous interreligious discussions from which I continue to learn. Dialogue with Christian partners and friends, in which we also grappled with racism and other structures of systemic injustice in Christian communities, has helped me to become aware of such structures within my own tradition and to hear the voices of the marginalized who experience my tradition as oppressive. On the constructive side, they help me discern the theological resources within the Hindu tradition that I could retrieve to show why we cannot be indifferent to injustice and to argue for relationships that affirm the equal dignity of every human being and exemplify compassion and justice. Through the eyes of my Christian friends, I see better both the interpretations and practices within my tradition that are oppressive and those that have the potential to liberate from oppression. In other words, I gain a better understanding of my own tradition.

Let me give an example, with one of my favorite Christian texts, to make clearer how this learning works for me, using the parable of the sheep and the goats in Matthew 25:31–46. In this parable, Jesus commends virtuous human beings as those who engage in acts of care and service toward the suffering. These are the ones who will be richly rewarded. His words, however, intrigue his hearers, since he uses the personal pronoun:

> For I was hungry and you gave me something to eat,
> I was thirsty and you gave me something to drink, I
> was a stranger and you invited me in, I needed clothes
> and you clothed me, I was sick and you looked after

me, I was in prison and you came to visit me. (Matt 25:35–36)

Puzzled, they ask,

> Lord, when did we see you hungry and feed you, or thirsty and give you something to drink? When did we see you a stranger and invite you in, or needing clothes and clothe you? When did we see you sick or in prison and go to visit you? (Matt 25:37–39)

The heart of the parable is in the response of Jesus to their perplexity:

> Truly I tell you, whatever you did for one of the least of these brothers and sisters of mine, you did for me.[11] (Matt 25:40–41)

This is one of my favorite Christian texts and one from which I learn deeply. I understand this parable to affirm the divine presence in every human being. This is a teaching that is also powerfully present in the Hindu tradition. Bhagavadgītā 13:28–29, for example, puts it in this way:

> *samaṁ sarveṣhu bhūteṣhu tiṣhṭhantaṁ parameśhvaram*
> *vinaśhyatsv avinaśhyantaṁ yaḥ paśhyati sa paśhyati*

> One who sees the Supreme God existing equally in all
>   beings,
> the imperishable in the perishable, truly sees.

The eighteenth and final chapter of the Bhagavadgītā (18:61) speaks of God as existing in the hearts of all beings (*īśhvaraḥ sarva-bhūtānāṁ hṛid-deśhe 'rjuna tiṣhṭhati*).

What Jesus makes powerfully clear, however, are the implications of this truth for human relationships. The truth of divine immanence is meant to promote certain kinds of actions—feeding the hungry, sheltering the homeless, offering hospitality to the stranger, visiting the lonely. The love of God, who is present equally in all, is not meaningful unless it moves us to care for those who suffer. The extraordinary and explicit way in which Jesus spells out this connection inspires me to ponder deeply the connection between the Hindu emphasis on divine immanence and social justice.

I have also thought more about religious ritual and justice. The most common form of Hindu worship in temples and homes, spoken of in Sanskrit as *pūja*, involves a series of hospitality offerings to God in the form of an icon, or *mūrti*. These offerings include many of the necessities mentioned by Jesus in the Matthew parable: welcoming into one's home, food, water, and clothing. Jesus's teaching intensifies the necessity for us to be mindful that the worship of God through ritual cannot be divorced from human relationships and especially our relationships with the "least" among us. If offering the necessities of life to a divine icon constitutes worship, so also is caring for the least among us, in whom God is present. The latter is even preferable.

A Hindu Theology of Liberation

My learning about theology and social justice is ongoing but reached a milestone in 2015 with the publication of my book *A Hindu Theology of Liberation*, in which I attempted, perhaps for the first time in the Hindu tradition, to articulate a systematic Hindu theology of liberation.[12] In many important ways, this work is a culminating point in the journey that started at Rajpur.

In the first half of this book, I outlined the theological building blocks for social justice. In the subsequent chapters, I applied these building blocks to a variety of contemporary issues that include patriarchy, homophobia, anthropocentrism, casteism, and the treatment of children. For each of these chapters, I can easily identify the dialogue meetings—some bireligious, between Hindus and Christians, and others multireligious—that inspired my learning, thinking, and writing.

More recently, during the years 2016–18, I have had the privilege of being a Hindu participant in a series of "Ethics in Action" meetings at the Vatican's Academy for Sciences in Rome. In the course of two years, we covered a wide variety of topics that included poverty, peace, migration, corporate responsibility, education, climate justice, modern slavery and human trafficking, corruption, and the future of work. Although I gave short presentations on each of these themes, I had no heritage of reflection on these subjects within the Hindu tradition to draw from. I benefited, however, from the history of Catholic social teaching to which I was introduced in a special way in these meetings. The rich history of Catholic reflection on human dignity, subsidiarity, the common good, and the dignity of work stimulated questions and opened windows into my own tradition. Catholic social teaching is concerned with applying fundamental teachings to the challenges of life in communities, and I continue to learn from this tradition as I think and write about the topics that we addressed in these "Ethics in Action" meetings. My principal conversation partners today are a few Hindus and my friends from the Christian and other traditions who are engaged in the theology and praxis of liberation. I am also learning from the experiences of oppressed persons within the Hindu tradition who have converted to other religions, many of them Christians, and who construct theology from the margins.

A Suffering God

I spoke earlier of the Hindu mode of worship that involves hospitality offerings made to God in icon or *mūrti* form. These can be anthropomorphic forms, representing the divine in the likeness of a human male or female; theriomorphic forms that combine human and animal features, like the divine as Ganesha; or abstract forms like the cylinder-shaped Shivalinga. Each of the major God representations—Vishnu, Shiva, and the divine feminine, Durga—has numerous forms as well as names.[13]

In addition, many Hindu traditions, especially those that center on God as Vishnu, affirm the teaching that God periodically assumes a form and enters our human world as an *avatāra*. Two of the well-known *avatāras* are Krishna and Rama. One of the key texts speaking of the nature and purpose of such a divine descent is Bhagavadgītā 4:7–8:

> Whenever there is a decline of righteousness and a rise of unrighteousness, then I manifest myself.
>
> For the protection of the virtuous, for the destruction of the evildoers, and for the establishment of righteousness, I am born from age to age.

These verses specify three purposes of the divine descent: the protection of the virtuous, the destruction of evildoers, and the establishment of righteousness.

In Hindu temples across the world, *mūrtis* (icons) of the *avatāras* and the principal representations of God are ritually installed and become the focus of Hindu ritual and worship. The Hindu temple is regarded as the abode of the divine, who is worshipped there as the King of kings or, in the case of feminine forms of God, as the Queen of queens. Large Hindu temples have priests who care for the icon and conduct the daily schedule of worship. Worship begins at dawn with soft, sacred music, followed by a ceremonial bath and anointment with sandal paste, new robes, ornaments, and flowers. Such procedures are called *pūja* and comprise numerous acts of hospitality extended to God in *murti* form.

The many forms and names of God in the Hindu tradition testify to an infinite divine who cannot be limited to a single form or name. These forms and names also speak to the multiple ways in which we encounter and experience the divine. Each form opens a window to see and experience some dimension of the inexhaustible divine. Each one is a *darśana*, a way of seeing and understanding the divine.

In the midst of this astonishing multiplicity of windows that reveal the nature of the divine, Jesus offers us a unique way of seeing. In its challenging difference, it is one from which we can learn deeply.

To put it simply, we do not have a divine embodiment or form in the Hindu tradition who is executed in pain and humiliation on a cross and who in anguish cries out to God, "Why have you abandoned me?" We do not have a God-figure who is whipped, stripped to his undergarments, made to wear a crown of thorns and carry his cross, and put to death with two thieves at his side. These radical differences led to Hindu doubts about crucifixion. Swami Vivekananda, who I cited earlier, denied its reality. "Christ was God incarnate; they could not kill him," said Vivekananda. "That which was crucified was only a semblance, a mirage."[14] We do not have a divine embodiment whose life does not end in victory. The life narratives of Rama and Krishna end with the defeat of tyrannical rulers. Jesus's end was in ignominy and humiliation. There is no divine intervention, no visible victory. To say the least, it is different.

What Can We Learn from a Crucified God?

What can Hindus learn here? The Christian tradition, as a whole, agrees that Jesus reveals to us the nature of God and the meaning of our humanity. At the heart of this twofold revelation is love (agape). He reveals the nature of God as love and the fullness of our humanity in love. First John 4:8 states it succinctly and beautifully: "Anyone who does not love does not know God, because God is love" (ESV).

The love of God is not unknown in the Hindu tradition. The Bhagavadgītā repeatedly uses the word *dear* (*priyaḥ*) to describe human beings in relation to God. Jesus's suffering, like a human being and for human beings, and his willingness to offer his life is an intense and powerful testimony of the passionate and personal depth and meaning of divine love that has no limits.

Jesus experienced God, the ground and source of all existence, as infinite love, and he responded with an obedient love that similarly had no boundaries and for which no sacrifice was too great. Jesus's suffering was not joyfully embraced. He prayed that he may be spared the cup of suffering and did so with an intensity that made his sweat fall like drops of blood. He experienced the anguish of feeling abandoned by God.

The fullness of this love left no room for hate. His was an example not just of nonviolence (*ahiṁsā*) but, positively, of love. In fact, we may say that in the case of Jesus, *ahiṁsā* was an outcome of love. In the absence of love, *ahiṁsā* is only an abstention from violence. It is this revelation of love, divine and human, that led Gandhi, a Hindu, to say to all Hindus "that your lives will be incomplete unless you reverently study the teachings of Jesus."[15] We can continue to learn from Jesus's distinctive embodiment and prioritizing of love and its meaning for human relationships. Love and *ahiṁsā* are complimentary and incomplete without the other. Hinduism prioritizes *ahiṁsā*;

Jesus prioritizes love. These virtues beautifully complement and complete each other.

Some of the major traditions of Hinduism characterize the human problem in the language of ignorance (*avidyā*). It is primarily an epistemological problem, since we are not separate by space or time from the infinite being that is God. This epistemological gap, as it were, is bridged by a transformative knowledge through which we discover our inseparability from the divine. The emphasis, therefore, is on knowledge (*jñāna*) as a process occurring in the mind. Jesus reminds us that this infinite being from whom we cannot be separate is a being of infinite love; our ignorance is also a separation of the heart from a love that enfolds us; our overcoming of ignorance, therefore, is an awakening to not only the unity of all in God but the unity of all in love. To awaken to love is to be transformed by love and to express love in all relationships, even when it hurts. This is what we must learn from Jesus.

Let me conclude on this theme of love with a comment that I think unites the different dimensions of learning from Christianity that I sought to identify in this chapter. The Hindu tradition, as I noted earlier, shares an understanding with Christianity of the love of God who is present in all and who embraces all beings. In the case of Jesus, however, this love is expressed in a very special concern. In Jesus, we see a preferential concern for those in our communities who suffer from inadequate access to life's necessities, from the abuse of power and privilege, or from social hierarchies that are exploitative and deny their dignity. These are our fellow human beings who suffer because of choices made and structures created by other human beings. Love requires that we strive to overcome suffering that has its roots in such injustice.

I believe that this preferential concern for the marginalized, the outcastes and the powerless, is uniquely expressed in the teachings and, even more, in the example of Jesus. In

Jesus, this becomes the measure of our religious commitment. Unfortunately, there are prominent interpretations of Hindu teachings that are summoned to justify a hierarchical caste ordering of human beings that has stripped millions of their dignity. It is a system that perpetuates unequal access to the material resources required for decent living and justifies social hierarchy with certain kinds of religious arguments. Jesus's teaching that divine love has a particular concern for the victims of injustice and that our love for one another must reflect this divine commitment is a message from which Hindus can and must learn. It may indeed be the place of our greatest learning.

CHAPTER SIX

What Can Christians Learn from Hinduism?

I want to begin this chapter with a confession. It is a much more difficult one for me to write than the previous chapter of this book focusing on Hindu learning from Christianity. In spite of the title of the chapter, my aim is not to authoritatively tell Christians what they should learn from Hinduism. I am not comfortable writing in this instructive mode. Learning from another tradition is a deep and slow process requiring humility, openness, discernment, trust, and empathy. It is an engagement of both head and heart. Interreligious learning is a journey of commitment in which one discovers, for oneself, the wisdom of another tradition that enriches one's religious life.

In addition, meaningful interreligious learning is always mutual. Gandhi spoke of this mutuality in powerful words to Christian missionaries that are applicable to people of all religions: "The powers of God should not be limited by the limitations of your understanding. To you who have come to teach India, I therefore say, you cannot give without taking. If you have come to give rich treasures of experiences, open your hearts out to receive the treasures of this land, and you will not be disappointed, neither will you have misread the message of the Bible."[1]

"You cannot give without taking." The words of Gandhi ring with truth. You cannot give your hand in greeting to another without receiving, and giving to another tradition requires the openness of receiving. Although my focus is on what Hindus may have to offer, I do so cognizant of the fact that we are also receivers from Christians who embody the teachings of Jesus. It is important that our acknowledgment of learning be mutual.

In the preceding chapter, I selectively identified Hindu teachers and leaders who acknowledged learning from Jesus. Among these were Rammohan Roy, Keshub Chandra Sen, Swami Vivekananda, and Mahatma Gandhi. Over thirty-five years ago, at the invitation of the World Council of Churches, I wrote an essay titled "A Hindu Looks at Jesus."[2] In my own case, it seems inevitable that I would know of Jesus from a very young age. I grew up in a Hindu family in Trinidad, a small island of ethnic, cultural, and religious diversity in the southern Caribbean. We were permitted to participate in nativity plays in kindergarten and to join our friends at the local church for Sunday school. I will always remember how elated I felt when I answered what seemed to be an incredibly difficult question. We were asked to guess how long Joseph knocked on the inn-keeper's door the night Jesus was born. Some of the unsuccess-ful answers attempted to quantify the number of knocks, while others gave a specific length of time. Suddenly, I intuitively yelled, "Until the door was opened," and I exulted in getting the answer that eluded my Christian friends and, of course, the prized treat!

Christian missionaries regularly called at our home to talk and to distribute literature. We politely listened, accepted, and occasionally read the material they left with us. At the Presbyterian high school where I received my secondary school education, there were further opportunities to hear of Jesus. I read the Gospels and also made an effort to better understand Hinduism through reading works by modern commentators, like Gandhi and Swami Vivekananda. I found the account of these writers full of admiration and warmth toward Jesus and the conviction of his importance. Such Hindu reflections sustained my interest in Jesus and helped me look beyond the missionary zeal and obsession for proselytization and the representation of Jesus as condemning all religions. They enabled me to look deeper into the meaning of his life and teachings and to discern both an affirmation and radical challenge to my own understanding of what it means to be religious. At an early age, Hindu interpreters, rather than Christian ones, were shaping my perception of Jesus more decisively. The foremost among these was Swami Vivekananda.

What powerfully attracted me to Jesus, and I believe attracted Hindus from the time of Rammohan Roy, is his unmistakable awakening to and centeredness in God. I found that the symbols and images, the examples and parables used by Jesus in talking about the religious life, had a lot in common with Hindu texts and teachers. His words and actions were infused with an authenticity that spoke immediately to one's heart. He exemplifies a direct mindfulness of God, an awareness of a deeper dimension to reality that is inviting and that anchors and gives meaning to existence. He embodies an intimate connectedness to this reality that is truer for him than anything else.

Through my Hindu eyes, I saw Jesus as living in and for God. His rootedness in God manifested itself in a life lived without fear of power and that, at depth, was full and peaceful. The fullness that Jesus experienced from his unity with God liberated him from greed and enabled him to live generously for others. This freedom was transparent in a lifestyle of nonpossessiveness, his teaching about the limits of wealth, and his condemnation of greed.

Jesus's understanding of God as infinite love, fullness, and peace and his conviction that God fulfills the deepest human longings explain his extraordinary compassion. Although God is the end of all human seeking, we repeatedly turn to unsatisfactory substitutes, failing to find the meaning that we search for and hurting our fellow beings and ourselves. Jesus's final words from the cross, "Father, forgive them; for they know not what they do" (Luke 23:32–34 KJV), never fail to move and draw me. This is more than a plea for forgiveness for those who did not acknowledge him. It is a prayer for all who are unable to realize the abundant potential of human existence and who choose violent ways of living. It reveals a heart of compassion that has no space for hate and that finds no delight in vengeful crushing of the other. The space between Jesus's vision of the human possibility and our failure to realize this is filled with an extraordinary love.

My deep interest in the Christian tradition is the consequence of growing up in a religiously diverse community, attending a Christian high school, teaching in the religion department at Saint Olaf College, and participating for more than forty years in Hindu-Christian dialogue under the auspices of the World Council of Churches, the Vatican's Pontifical Council for Inter-religious Dialogue, and other major organizations.

My aim in this chapter is to identify some significant insights from the Hindu tradition that may open doors to deeper dialogue, learning, and mutual enrichment. I do not claim that Hindus have always been faithful to these insights, and I do not suggest the superiority of one tradition over the other.

It is important that we keep in mind that we are discussing two world religions that exemplify considerable internal diversity. This diversity makes generalizations hazardous. In the case of the Hindu tradition, the diversity is extensive and ancient. The term *Hindu* has a geographical origin and is connected with the name of the river that we now know as the Indus. *Hindu* is one variation in the pronunciation of the river's name. It is not the personal name of a founder and does not point to a single teaching or practice. It is an umbrella term that shelters an astonishing variety of teachings and practices specific to microtraditions (*saṁpradāyas*). I emphasize this fact because, although there are shared teachings and practices, there are also exclusive theological claims within the Hindu tradition that are difficult to reconcile with each other. Hindus are not a homogenous group, and Hinduism is misleading if we assume uniformity. One does not learn from Hinduism; one learns from specific Hindu traditions and teachers. Similarly, given the theological diversity of the Christian tradition, it will not surprise me at all to learn that a Hindu teaching that I commend is already present, in some form, in a particular Christian tradition.

My suggestions are drawn broadly from the Hindu tradition but most specifically from the tradition of nonduality, known as *Advaita*. This is the tradition of my personal commitment and primary scholarship. Advaita, which literally means "not-two," is one of many Hindu traditions that regard the four Vedas as authoritative sources of religious teaching. Advaita considers the dialogues between teachers and students found at the end of each Veda, and known as the Upaniṣads, to contain the highest teachings of the texts. These dialogues are the focus of traditional study and commentary.

I will organize my discussion under three themes: (1) the God-universe relationship, (2) the human problem, and (3) liberation.

God-Universe Relationship

Let me start where most of the dialogues of the Upaniṣads begin, which is with the origin of the universe. Upaniṣad accounts of creation begin with the existence of a single, undivided, infinite reality, referred to as *brahman*. Here are two texts:

> Om. In the beginning this was but the one self alone. There was nothing else whatsoever that winked. It thought "Let me create the worlds." (Aitareya Upaniṣad 1.1.1)[3]

> In the beginning, dear boy, this was Being alone, one
> only, without a second. (Chāndogya Upaniṣad 6.2.1)

In both of these texts, we see the concern to emphasize the reality of the One alone, and nothing other than the One, before creation. The Upaniṣads reject explicitly the origin of the universe from nonexistence. The Chāndogya Upaniṣad 6.2.2 asks the question, "How can what is existent be born from what is non-existent?"

The rejection of dualism before creation and the affirmation of one indivisible divine being are theological claims shared broadly by Hinduism and Christianity. In the words of Rowan Williams, former archbishop of Canterbury, "God is the unique source of everything. . . . There is nothing alongside God, nothing by nature extra to God or beyond God. God is never one thing among other things."[4]

For both traditions, the One alone is the sovereign source of all that exists. There is no other reality, material or otherwise, coeternal with God out of which God creates or by which God is assisted. The universe is totally dependent, moment to moment, on God for its existence.

In explaining the origin of the universe from God, the unanimous Christian teaching is "creation out of nothing" (*creatio ex nihilo*), a phrase used as early as the second century. Although rejecting, as we have seen, any dualism prior to creation, the Hindu tradition has not employed the language of creation out of nothing. The Upaniṣads speak of the One as bringing forth the many out of itself, employing a metaphor of self-multiplication. Here are two relevant Upaniṣad texts:

> He wished, "Let me be many, let me be born." He under-
> took a deliberation. Having deliberated, he created all
> this that exists. That (Brahman) having created (that),
> entered into that very thing. (Taittirīya Upaniṣad 2.6.1)

> That Being willed, "May I become many, may I grow
> forth." (Chāndogya Upaniṣad 6.2.3)

This language is quite different from Christian creation narratives, and it has resulted in many Christian interpreters describing the Hindu worldview as pantheistic. I am using pantheism to describe a theology in which the creator literally becomes the creation and is equated fully with it. In other words, the creator is nothing more than the creation. Such a simple identification of creator and creation, unfortunately, misrepresents Hindu theologies.

Although consistently describing the universe as emerging from the being of God with the metaphors of self-multiplication and expansion, the Upaniṣads do not naively equate creator and creation. As the famous invocation verse of the Bṛhadāraṇyaka Upaniṣad (5.1.1) reminds us, the universe that emerges from the divine neither adds to nor subtracts from divine infinity. After bringing forth all things, the divine remains full and inexhaustible (*pūrṇamevavaśiṣyate*).[5] The One transcends everything finite and all efforts to comprehensively define and describe it. We can speak of it only with wonder and of the universe as the overflow of inexhaustible divine abundance.

What are the theological implications of describing the creation as divine self-multiplication, brought forth from the being of and existing only in God? These outcomes are explicit in almost every Hindu sacred text. Fundamentally, it fills us with the deepest reverence for every being and every created form. As Bhagavadgītā 13:27 puts it, "One who sees the Supreme God existing equally in all beings, the imperishable in the perishable, truly sees."

These words admit to no exclusions and no distinctions. Put simply, God exists equally in all beings. The indivisible infinite cause is present in every created effect. The divine presence is not limited by anything—nation, gender, ethnicity, religion, or age. This is the source of the intrinsic dignity of every human being. Every human encounter is a meeting with the divine, and we are reminded of this in the traditional greeting "Namaste." The root verb, *namati*, means to bow, to recognize and remember that one stands in the presence of divinity.

It is important, however, to emphasize that the dignity of creation is not anthropocentric. Bhagavadgītā 7:8–9 invites us to see the infinite in the taste of water, in the brilliance of light in the moon and sun, in the pure fragrance of the earth, and in the radiance of fire. The Śvetāśvatāra Upaniṣad (4:3) speaks of divinity in "the dark blue bird, the green one with red eyes, the rain-cloud, the seasons and the oceans." History and sacred texts are not the only places where we encounter the divine; it must also be seen in the natural world. Creation expresses and celebrates the divine.

These Hindu teachings are beautifully articulated in the opening verse of the Īśa Upaniṣad:

> *īśāvāsyamidaṃ sarvaṃ yatkiñca jagatyāṃ jagat* |
> *tena tyaktena bhuñjīthā mā gṛdhaḥ kasyasviddhanam*

> This entire universe, moving and unmoving, is
>   enfolded in God.
> Renounce and enjoy. Do not covet the wealth of
>   others.

The first line affirms the truth of God—named here as *īśa*, ruler or lord—and describes the universe as enfolded or wrapped in the divine (*īśāvāsyam*). Nothing and no one are outside of God; nothing exists separate from God. Enfolding is a form of embracing and suggests care and love. It points also to the precious worth of the universe that is enfolded in God as a child in the hands of a mother or father. The text invites us to see the universe as a sacred reality that exists within God and is sustained continuously by God. Such seeing in the Hindu tradition is spoken of as *darśana* or sacred seeing.

Darśana is seeing the familiar with new eyes; it is the restoration of sacredness and mystery to what we regard as ordinary. It is to walk with every step on sacred ground. I regard it as a significant theological lack if a tradition does not offer an understanding of the divine-universe relationship that evokes reverence and care for sentient beings and the universe and does not also lift up the implied ethical obligations that follow. In rediscovering reverence for the universe, I believe that Christians can learn from the wisdom of the Hindu tradition.

The Methodist Christian theologian Diana Eck made important observations about her tradition that speak to this issue after her encounter with Hinduism. She raised a significant question:

> There is no part of nature that carries for Christians the cultural power and mythic energy of the Ganges as much as I love the Madison, the Gallatin, and the Blackfoot rivers. Why not? Perhaps those of us in the Western prophetic traditions have been afraid that we will worship nature and not God. After all the prophets of Israel embarked on a bold religious venture—to see the mighty power of God not in the mysteries of nature, as did their neighbors in the ancient world, but in the mystery of historical events. . . . But "nature" and "history" are not true opposites. Do we really need to choose one and not the other?[6]

Hindus do not feel the need to choose; we are limited only by our inability to see. The implications for ecological sustainability of such a reverence for the natural world are matters that Hindus and Christians could together pursue. There are many biblical texts that could enrich such a dialogue. One of my favorites is Psalm 139: "Where can I go from Your Spirit? Or where can I flee from Your presence? If I ascend into heaven, You *are* there; If I make my bed in hell, behold, You *are there*. If I take the wings of the morning, *And* dwell in the uttermost parts of the sea, Even there Your hand shall lead me, And Your right hand shall hold me" (Ps 139:7–10 NKJV).[7] In Acts 17:27–28, we have Paul's emphasis on the immediacy of God: "They would search for God and perhaps grope for [God] and find [God]—though indeed [God] is not far from each one of us. For 'In [God] we live and move and have our being'" (NRSV). Such passages reveal an omnipresent divine who is present in every created form and who is found in every space.

The Human Problem

One of my favorite verses in the Bhagavadgītā comes from the sixth chapter (30): "For those who see me everywhere and see all things in me, I am never lost, nor are they ever lost to me" (*yo mām pashyati sarvatra / sarvaṁ cha mayi pashyati / tasyāham na pranashyāmi / sa cha me na pranashyati*). The Kaṭha Upaniṣad (1.2.20) describes the divine as being smaller than the smallest and larger than the largest, residing in the heart of all beings (*anoraniyānmahato mahīyanātmāsyajantornihitoguhāyām*).

The point consistently made across the Hindu traditions is that we are not and cannot ever be separate in any spatial or temporal sense from God. This is true, whether we know it or not. For this reason, the Hindu tradition has described the human problem in a way that is different from most Christian traditions. It speaks of this problem as one of ignorance (*avidyā*). Human nature is not fundamentally flawed or corrupted, but our understanding of ourselves is clouded. Under the condition of ignorance, we are not aware that we share the fullness of the divine, bigger than the biggest and smaller than the smallest, present at the core of everything and in our own hearts. It is this fullness that we truly seek and that alone will satisfy us.

The consequences of ignorance are not to be minimized. These are far-reaching and produce considerable suffering, individually and socially. The Upaniṣads speak of ignorance as one of the three knots of the heart (*hṛdayagranthi*) from which one must be free. The three knots are ignorance, greed, and greedy actions (*avidyā-kāma-karma*). Ignorant of the fullness of the divine that we share and that unites us with all creation, we regard ourselves as incomplete, inadequate, lacking, and separate. The sense of inadequacy and incompleteness that results from ignorance causes the multiplication of desires—in other words, greed—in an effort to overcome this condition of lack. We seek continuously to bolster up and secure the self. We exert ourselves for ends such as wealth, fame, and power beyond reasonable needs, hoping that the gain of these will free us from self-inadequacy and anxiety. Such gains are short-lived and leave us in a condition of want and dissatisfaction. Greed is egocentric and socially harmful, since it leads to hurtful consequences and to structures that cause suffering for others.

Returning to describing the human problem, we may say that it is fundamentally epistemological, but with grave consequences at every level of existence. Our separation from God is a problem of not knowing. To discover the fullness of God in which we have our being, we need help. This help takes the form of a compassionate teacher through whose guidance we discover the truth of ourselves. The Chāndogya Upaniṣad (6.14.2) likens the person under the condition of ignorance to someone forcibly taken away from his beloved home, blindfolded, and left in the wilderness. A kind person answers his plea for help, removes his blindfold, and shows him the way home. In a similar manner, a compassionate teacher liberates the *avidyā*-bound individual.

Both the Hindu and Christian traditions propose a problem to be overcome but describe these differently. For the Christian tradition, the emphasis is on original sin, not ignorance. Because of sin, we live in a fallen state from which we need help to be saved. We cannot save ourselves. The consequences of sin and ignorance, however, are quite similar: egocentrism, fragmentation, greed, separation, and alienation. How could thinking about the human problem as one of original ignorance complement or enrich Christian thinking about original sin? What would it mean to know that we are never separate from God, that no misdeed can keep us from God, that God is always here and now? That what we need is an awakening through right understanding that reveals the ever-present God and the fundamental goodness of human nature?

The Īśa Upaniṣad (6) teaches that one who sees God in all and all in God will not hate. To be awake to God is to embrace every being in love. The text uses the language of the ultimate self (*ātmā*) as synonymous for God or *Īśa*, used in verse one. This is to emphasize the reality of God as the deepest truth of each self:

> The person who sees the self in all beings
> and all beings in the self does not hate anyone.

> *yastu sarvāni bhūtānyātmanyevānupaśyati*
> *sarvabhūteṣu cātmāna tato na vijugupsate*

The Christian theologian Marcus Borg rejects supernatural theism that advocates for an understanding of the divine "out there" and advocates instead for a biblical panentheism.[8] In Borg's view, the fusion of supernatural theism and monarchical images of God emphasizes meeting requirements, sin, and guilt.[9] Panentheism, on the other hand, which understands God as a nonmaterial reality, immanent and transcendent, sees the human problem in terms of estrangement and separation. In Borg's words, it is "our blindness to the presence of God, our separation from the Spirit who is all around us and within us and to which we belong."[10] We are not spatially but epistemologically distant from God. Christians who are interested in developing a theology along the lines suggested by Borg may benefit from engagement with the sacred texts and traditions of Hinduism.

Liberation

Finally, some words on liberation (*mokṣa*). The understanding that I sketched of the fundamental human problem has significant implications for thinking about the meaning of liberation and mutual learning between Hindus and Christians. When the human problem is one of ignorance and not one of spatial or temporal separation from God, then liberation, like God, is also here and now. Liberation—or freedom as it is more properly called in Hindu traditions—does not await, especially in the nondual teachings, the death of the physical body or require a journey to another world. It is synonymous with the overcoming of ignorance. Several Hindu traditions speak, therefore, of the state of living liberation (*jīvanmukti*) and of the living liberated (*jīvanmukta*).

Since liberation is awakening to the reality of the divine that is present equally in all beings and at the heart of each self, it is regarded as an end that is already accomplished. Liberation is not the fruit of human action that, being finite, can only produce a finite result. It is not the consequence of any human effort. It is not a created product. There is effort involved, but this is more in the nature of removing the ignorance or false understanding and the negative dispositions of mind and heart that obscure our true seeing and understanding. We do not create what we see—we remove the impediments to seeing. When the Īśa Upaniṣad (1) speaks of seeing the world wrapped in God (*īśāvāsyamidaṃ sarvaṃ*), the text is speaking of an existing reality and not of one that has to be brought into being. We are invited to see what is here and now and not what is yet to come. The teaching on living liberation does not imply that liberation is without postmortem implications. The point here is that any such outcomes after the death of the body follow from the state of liberation in life (*jīvanmukti*). Liberation is not an end that must await the death of the body, since the human problem is synonymous not with the fact of being alive but with ignorance of God.

On the whole, Hindu texts demonstrate a preference for speaking about liberation here and now and about the implications of liberation for our lives in this world. One of the most significant fruits of the new understanding of self that follows the overcoming of ignorance is freedom from greed. Ignorance is associated with self-lack and anxiety about self-worth. Liberation, on the other hand, that reveals the fullness of the divine that we all share frees us from greed and self-centeredness. In contrast with greed, desire-multiplication, and selfishness—which are all associated with ignorance—liberation is synonymous with a deep identification with all beings and with compassion and generosity. The liberated is consistently described as one who sees herself in all beings or one who sees the divine equally present in all. She identifies with all in both suffering and happiness and finds delight in their flourishing (Bhagavadgītā 5:25; 12:4; 6:32): "One who identifies herself equally with all beings, in happiness and suffering, is the best Yogi" (*ātmaupamyena sarvatra / samaṃ paśyati yo 'rjuna / sukhaṃ vā yadi vā duḥkhaṃ sa yogī paramo mataḥ* [6:32]).

This identification with all beings transcends the boundaries of nationality, religion, race, sex, and ethnicity. Hating and oppressing others on the basis of caste, sex, or race is unjust and a consequence of blindness to the truth of life's unity. Positively, the identity with all expresses itself in the practice of compassion (*dayā*), generosity (*dāna*), and commitment to the public good (*lokasaṅgraham*).

This Hindu emphasis on liberation here and now, in this world, could be a meaningful place for Hindu-Christian learning and dialogue. Although there are Christian theologies, with liberation theology as an outstanding contemporary example, that speak more prominently about the significance of life in this world, the major emphasis is on the life to come. Living liberation implies that even with all the challenges of life in the world, the divine is present and always available. The encounter with the divine does not have to await a future moment; it is not future-oriented but centered on the present and on life in this world. Knowing this, we may strive more diligently to overcome those causes that impede us from seeing this reality now.

A renewed emphasis on the divine here and now provides a deeper motivation for ethical action in the world. Values that I identified earlier, such as compassion and generosity, are not instrumental to future reward or attainment but express the most profound meaning of liberation. Embodying compassion and justice is how we are when we are awake to the divine. Liberation is a way of being, not a future reward.

Conclusion

To conclude, let me return to the opening verse of the Īśa Upaniṣad:

> *īśāvāsyamidaṃ sarvaṃ yatkiñca jagatyāṃ jagat |*
> *tena tyaktena bhuñjīthā mā gṛdhaḥ kasyasviddhanam*

> This entire universe, moving and unmoving, is
>   enfolded in God.
> Renounce and enjoy. Do not covet the wealth of
>   others.

I already commented on the significance of the first line: seeing the universe enfolded in God. The final line identifies at least two outcomes of this liberated understanding. The liberated way of seeing the universe as unceasingly embraced by God is presented here as a mode of renunciation (*tyaktena*). It is the giving up of desires to possess, dominate, and instrumentalize the world as existing only to serve human purposes and instead cultivating care, responsibility, and noninjury. The world has intrinsic value and embodies the divine. Paradoxically, the renunciation of greed that is associated with instrumentalizing the world results in a deeper delight (*bhuñjīthā*). Giving up greed enhances joy. The world is the place where we can know and celebrate divinity with joy.

Similarly, freedom from covetousness speaks of a transformation in human relationships from rivalry and competitiveness to unity, cooperation, reverence, and intrinsic value. One's worth as a human being is not dependent on the devalued worth of another. We can rejoice, as the Bhagavadgītā teaches, in the flourishing of every being.

The Bhagavadgītā (12:13) speaks of the one dear to God as compassionate, forgiving, friendly, and without hate and selfishness. It commends identifying with others in suffering and happiness (6:32) and finding delight in working for the flourishing of others (12:4). In both of our traditions, the self-centered religious life is a contradiction. The highest teachings of our tradition do not turn us away from our neighbors in need or deafen us to their cries. Our understanding of God is not true unless it finds active expression in lives of loving compassion and in work that aims to alleviate suffering. We understand the service of others as a humble privilege and opportunity to serve God. Hindus and Christians, who see the significance of liberation for our lives in this world, could help each other understand deeper and better the obligations of our religious commitments and together strive for the overcoming of suffering and injustice in our world.

We can stand together and join our voices against any ideology and political or social structure that denies the personhood and dignity of human beings and that condones injustice and irreverence. We can speak together for justice and do so for reasons that include but go beyond the political and economic—we can speak of the divine presence in the heart of the human. Today, the discernment of this divine presence calls us with urgency to reverence for our common home, the earth, to united efforts to halt its degradation, and to promote ecological responsibility in our nations, communities, and corporations. In these tasks, Christians and Hindus can learn from each other and labor joyfully together.

The Political and the Theological

Why Hindu-Christian Dialogue?

In various chapters of this book, I identified reasons for Hindu-Christian dialogue and suggested ways in which such dialogue may go forward and be mutually enriching. The traditions of Hinduism and Christianity together claim at least 3.2 billion followers around the world.[1] Given the benefits of dialogue to our world community, it would be a tragic loss if such dialogue failed to occur because of indifference, hostility, or fear.

Our world has always been religiously diverse, both across and within religious traditions. Human beings have professed different beliefs and engaged in different practices for as long as we know. Religious diversity has not suddenly become a characteristic of our present age. What is new about our religious diversity is the fact that it is rapidly becoming a feature of many societies where diversity was limited or internal to a particular religion. Our awareness of other religions has never been as great as it is today.

The religious map of the United States, for example, as Diana Eck reminds us, has been and continues to be radically transformed by the opening of its doors to immigrants from Asia.[2] Until the latter half of the twentieth century, the borders of the United States were significantly shut to immigrants from Asia. The Chinese Exclusion Act of 1882 was gradually extended to include Filipinos, the Japanese, Koreans, and people of Indian origin. The preference for immigrants of European origin was formalized in the National Origins Act of 1924, which stipulated permanent restrictions on immigration from outside the Western world and prevented the entry of aliens not qualified for US citizenship. Such restrictions on immigration from Asia continued through the second World War. In 1965, a new immigration law, initiated by John F. Kennedy, abolished quotas based on national origins and opened the United States to immigrants from Asia. Today a Hindu, Buddhist, or Muslim can find a place of worship, prayer, or meditation in almost every major city in the United States, and there are growing communities of Sikhs, Jains, and Zoroastrians. When the Hindu teacher Swami Vivekananda traveled across the United States in 1893, he delivered most of his addresses to Christian audiences in Unitarian Churches. If Vivekananda visited the United States today, he could sit in Hindu temples and address the children and grandchildren of Hindu immigrants.

We cannot think of the religious diversity in our communities as a temporary phenomenon. We are growing in the realization, some more slowly than others, that this diversity is here to stay. There are no realistic prospects that human beings will be brought under a single tradition. Our modern era is witness to a new vitality and resurgence in many of our traditions. Many have emerged from colonialism with a renewed sense of purpose and universal relevance. They are ready to share their insights and to participate in the shaping of our world. I mention this fact because our willingness, as Hindus and Christians, to enter into relationships will depend, in part, on how realistic we are about the fact of religious diversity and whether we perceive this diversity as an unwelcome problem to be overcome or as an opportunity for enrichment, growth, and even religious revitalization. In an earlier chapter, I mentioned that Hindu-Christian dialogue is not served if Christians in India are viewed as an alien and unwelcome community. Dialogue is not consistent with wishing for the disappearance of people of other religions.

We live in communities that are radically and self-consciously diverse and, for all that we can see, are determined to stay so. In these communities, our lives are each day rapidly becoming intertwined with those of people of other faiths. We will all live our lives—religious, social, and professional—in the context of religious diversity. What W. C. Smith wrote decades ago is even more true today: "No longer, are people of other persuasions peripheral or distant, the idle curiosities of travelers' tale. The more alert we are, and the more involved in life, the more we are finding that they are our neighbors, our colleagues, our competitors, our fellows. Confucians and Hindus, Buddhist and Muslims, are with us not only in the United Nations, but down the street. Increasingly, not only is our civilization's destiny affected by their actions, but we drink coffee with them personally as well."[3]

Suffering and the Necessity for Interreligious Action

All of our religious traditions, in addition to what they teach about individual human destiny, also have a social vision of the ideal human community, characterized by justice, peace, prosperity, and freedom from violence, exploitation, and fear.

Any religious tradition that is today concerned about the social order and its transformation is challenged to reach across historical borders, find common ground and values with people of other faiths, and strive together to confront and overcome the causes of human suffering and conflict. Our hopes for just and peaceful communities will only be realized together or not at all. Interreligious cooperation and action are not a luxury for the starry-eyed among us but have become a real and practical necessity in our communities of diversity. In the task of community building, we must be ready to labor with women and men of every faith and with those who have none.

At our Hindu-Christian dialogue meeting in Rajpur, India (1981), "Religious Resources for a Just Society," we spoke of the need for dialogue on the shared problems in our communities and cooperative action in concrete projects to overcome injustice and violence and to address causes of human suffering.[4] Unfortunately, the promises of our meeting were not realized; these deserve our recommitment. The overcoming of suffering in this world, occasioned by lack of the basic necessities for decent living, socioeconomic oppression, violence, and ecological degradation, must be among the foremost reasons for Hindu-Christian dialogue. Paul Knitter reminds us that this liberation "cannot be realized piecemeal, in this or that culture or nation, but must be a worldwide, interconnected effort," requiring "a new dialogue among religions worldwide."[5]

I believe that the fundamental teachings of our traditions, Hindu and Christian, call us to this work together. In 2015, I was invited to present at a Georgetown University conference celebrating the fiftieth anniversary of Vatican II, an ecumenical council convened by Pope John XXIII to discuss doctrinal issues. In my presentation, I focused on "Gaudium et spes" (joy and hope), one of the significant documents emerging from Vatican II. "Gaudium et spes" spoke of a special concern for the poor and of the violation of justice and human dignity when there are excessive economic differences among people. "Gaudium et spes" was a major inspiration for the development of liberation theologies that emphasized an expansive understanding of liberation to include freedom from political, economic, religious, and social oppression.

The vision of a just human community, articulated in Vatican II, is not limited to Christianity. Other religious traditions offer hope for a world community characterized by justice, peace, prosperity, and freedom from fear and violence.

As noted above, in the interreligious and interrelated context of our lives, the pursuit of such visions calls us to cooperation across religious boundaries. Any religion that shares the concerns for overcoming suffering caused by poverty and oppression is challenged to reach across historical borders, search for common ground, and strive together for human flourishing. Our hopes for justice and peace will only be realized together. Interreligious praxis is a necessity of our times.

The inspiration of Vatican II and Christian liberation theology resonates in important ways in the teachings of the Hindu tradition and in the interpretations of some of its most prominent teachers. There is no glorification of involuntary poverty in the Hindu tradition. *Artha* (economic well-being) is one of the four fundamental goals of human life, along with pleasure, commitment to ethical conduct, and liberation. In the most popular version of the Rāmāyaṇa, the life story of Rama, the great Hindi poet Tulasidās speaks of poverty as the greatest suffering. His ideal human community is one in which no one is poor, illiterate, or diseased. One of the most famous Hindu teachers in recent times, Swami Vivekananda (1863–1902), coined the expression *daridra nārāyaṇa* (God as the poor) to call attention to the special claims of the poor on our attention and resources. In ways similar to the call of Vatican II to hear Christ in the suffering of the poor, Vivekananda appealed to Hindus to see Shiva in the poor and equated the service of the poor with the true worship of God: "He who sees Shiva in the poor, in the weak and in the diseased, really worships Shiva; and if he sees Shiva only in the image, his worship is but preliminary."[6]

Mahatma Gandhi spoke repeatedly of the interrelatedness of all dimensions of human life. One could not separate the social, political, economic, or religious dimensions of human existence into impermeable compartments. All these fields of action are concerned with human well-being. Gandhi foreshadowed one of the defining orientations of liberation theology, referred to as the "preferential option for the poor": "I count no sacrifice too great for the sake of seeing God face to face. The whole of my activity whether it may be called social, political, humanitarian or ethical is directed to that end. And as I know that God is found more often in the lowliest of His creatures than in the high and mighty, I am struggling to reach the status of these. I cannot do so without their service. Hence my passion for the service of the suppressed classes."[7]

We remember Gandhi as the great advocate of nonviolence (*ahiṃsā*). In his explanation of *ahiṃsā*, however, he was always careful to clarify that its meaning was not negative. *Ahiṃsā* means love and compassion for all; it also means the practice of justice and freedom from exploitation. "No man," wrote Gandhi, "could be actively non-violent and not rise against social injustice no matter where it occurred."[8]

Both of our traditions are challenged by theological interpretations that are not attentive to the significance of life in this world and even encourage indifference to the world and its concerns. Such interpretations lead to understandings of the meaning of liberation that equate it with freedom from the world. In the Hindu tradition, the primary meaning of liberation then becomes freedom from the cycle of birth, death, and rebirth, or freedom from the world. Liberation is disconnected from our lives here and now. Such interpretations of the significance of the world, life in the world, and the meaning of liberation are not the only ones available in the Hindu tradition and reflect specific historical readings of its sacred sources. There are alternative readings that propose a greater value for the world and offer a vision of a liberated life that put the emphasis on a transformed way of being and new relationships here and now. These are world-affirming theologies that do not devalue the world or equate liberation with freedom from the world.[9]

In such theologies, liberation does not alienate us from life in community but draws us into a deeper unity with all. One is awake to life's unity in God or, as the Bhagavadgītā (18:20) puts it, to seeing the undivided divine in the midst of all divisions. The most important implication of this unitive seeing is owning the joy and suffering of others as one's own. The Bhagavadgītā speaks repeatedly of the liberated as "delighting in the wellbeing of others" (5:25; 12:4) and of identifying with others in suffering and in joy (6:32). Another way of speaking about this unity and identity with others is compassion (*karuṇa/dayā*). We must assume that this identification with others in suffering is not limited to emotional empathy. Our identification with others in suffering requires that we properly inquire into the causes of their suffering with the aim of overcoming these. The traditional emphasis has been on suffering as an inward condition, but there is no reason to limit the meaning of suffering in this way. Hindu texts commending the identification with others in suffering do not suggest any such limitation. What we need then is an expansive understanding of suffering and liberation. We cannot ignore the suffering of human beings when they lack opportunities to attain the necessities for dignified and decent living or when suffering is inflicted through oppression and injustice based on gender, birth, or race. It is not acceptable to affirm teachings about life's unity while being indifferent to inequality and oppression at the social level. Working to overcome suffering means identifying those political, social, and economic structures that cause and perpetuate suffering. The unmistakable call to be one with the suffering other requires nothing less.

Hindus and Christians can stand on common ground in affirming a human dignity and worth that springs from the divine presence in the human. In our distinctive ways, we hold the ultimately valuable One to be present in every human being. This living out of this truth requires work to overcome structures of inequality, indignity, and injustice. For both of our traditions, the life of generosity and compassion expresses best the meaning of liberation. Our response to human need is a response to God. Jesus's parable in Matthew 25:31–36 of the separation of the sheep and goats speaks of him as incarnate in the needy: "Truly I tell you, whatever you did for one of the least of these brothers and sisters of mine, you did for me" (Matt 25:40).

Inspired perhaps by this famous parable, Swami Vivekananda, at the Rameshwaram temple in 1897, also related a parable about the meaning of the religious life:

> A rich man had a garden and two gardeners. One of these gardeners was very lazy and did not work; but when the owner came to the garden, the lazy man would get up and fold his arms and say, "How beautiful is the face of my master," and dance before him. The other gardener would not talk much, but would work hard, and produce all sorts of fruits and vegetables which he would carry on his head to his master who lived a long way off. Of these two gardeners, which one would be the more beloved of his master? Shiva is that master, and this world is His garden, and there are two sorts of gardeners here; the one who is lazy, hypocritical, and does nothing, only talking about Shiva's beautiful eyes and nose and other features; and the other, who is taking care of Shiva's children, all those that are poor and weak, all animals, and all His creation. Which of these would be the more beloved of Shiva? Certainly, he that serves His children. He who wants to serve the father must serve the children first. He who wants to serve Shiva must serve His children—must serve all creatures in this world first. It is said in the Shastra that

those who serve the servants of God are His greatest servants.[10]

Speaking of this theological common ground is not meant to overlook or minimize the differences between the Hindu and Christian traditions. But this common ground is not insignificant, and I regard these as insights present at the heart of our traditions. It is a place that enables us to meet and speak with each other and, most importantly, act together for the flourishing of all. We can stand together and join our voices against any ideology and political or social structure that denies the personhood and dignity of human beings and that condones injustice and irreverence. We can speak together for justice and do so for reasons that include but go beyond the political and economic—we can speak of the divine presence at the heart of the human. Today, the discernment of this divine presence calls us with urgency to reverence for our common home, the earth; to united efforts to halt its degradation; and to promote ecological responsibility in our nations, communities, and corporations.

The highest teachings of our traditions do not turn us away from our neighbors in need or deafen us to their cries. Our traditions, in their distinctive insights, enable us to stand together for the dignity and equal worth of human beings. Our traditions enable us to stand together against injustice and the commodification of human life. Our traditions inspire us, in special ways, to lives of compassion and service for the overcoming of suffering in our world. In a world that longs for freedom from suffering, these are among the finest places, even in the midst of our differences, where Hindus and Christians can and should stand together in action and dialogue.

Theological Grounds for Dialogue

The arguments for Hindu-Christian dialogue advanced so far in this chapter are primarily, though not exclusively, political. In the interrelated circumstances of our lives, dialogue and cooperation are necessities for our well-being and for addressing our shared social and economic problems. They are an antidote to ignorance, fear, and dehumanization, which are the precursors of violence. In the words of S. Wesley Ariarajah, "Dialogue is not an ambulance service; it is a public health programme!" It is "an attempt to help people to understand and accept the other in their 'otherness.'" It seeks to make people "at home" with plurality, to develop an appreciation of diversity, and to make those links that may just help them hold together when the whole community is threatened by forces of separation and anarchy.[11]

Political arguments for dialogue, though necessary, are not sufficient. These are often articulated in ways that reduce the reasons for dialogue to pragmatic arguments. Though obvious, what distinguishes interreligious dialogue from other types of conversation is the fact that we are engaging one another from the depths of our religious commitments. Surely, the nature of these commitments must inform the fundamental reasons we reach out to our neighbors of other faiths. Without theological arguments, other traditions may have instrumental value for us; we are content as long as they maintain the peace and do not disrupt our lives. We have no reasons, however, to celebrate their presence among us. Pragmatic justifications for dialogue may bring us to tolerance for one another; such arguments do not give us reasons for theological celebration.

Several years ago, I articulated, in a series of questions, the challenges of theological arguments for dialogue:

> We begin to think theologically about religious diversity when we ask, not about the political value of others,

but about their religious value. What is the religious value of having a world in which there are Hindus, Muslims, Buddhists, Jews, Christians, Sikhs, Jains and Indigenous Peoples? How is our world diminished in the absence of any one of these? Do we have a religious need for each other? As a Hindu, what is my theological value to you? Does it matter to you religiously that there are Hindus in the world? Would it make any difference to you if there were no Hindus? Such questions are not easy ones to answer, but they are certainly among the most important ones that we can ask today in the context of our encounter with people of other religions. Each tradition will have to pursue these questions in its own distinctive ways.[12]

Interreligious dialogue, when done well, certainly fosters mutual learning and helps us better understand our own religious commitments. In the light of another tradition, we see more clearly the significance of our theological claims. We may even gain insights that enrich our understanding of divine nature and the religious life. Such arguments, however, do not challenge, fundamentally, religious claims for self-sufficiency and the absence of a need for one another. The question remains: What is the theological significance and need of persons of other faiths? Why is our world better because of religious diversity? Answers to such questions are important if the justification for dialogue must transcend the political. Such answers must emerge uniquely from each tradition, and dialogue would enable traditions to offer and develop such responses.

Interreligious Learning

My commitment as a Hindu scholar and practitioner is to the tradition of Advaita Vedānta. *Advaita* (lit. "not-two") is an exegetical tradition based on a reading of the Upaniṣads, which constitute the final sections of the four Vedas. The tradition looks to a line of distinguished teachers for the interpretation of these texts and for the transmission of its teachings. The most distinguished among these is Śaṅkara (ca. seventh century CE), who wrote extensive commentaries on the Upaniṣads and who is credited with the legacy of the finest systematic exposition of Advaita. The core Advaita truth claims are twofold. First, the infinite *brahman* constitutes the truth or ground of the universe in a way that is analogically similar to clay constituting the nature of all clay products. The relationship between *brahman* and everything else is best described as not-two. This is different from describing the relationship as one or two.[13] Second, the human self (*ātmā*) is identical with *brahman*.

The Advaita tradition offers a diagnosis of the human problem as one of suffering, identifies ignorance of the nature of the self (*ātmā*) as the fundamental cause of suffering, proposes liberation from ignorance (*mokṣa*) as the highest purpose of human existence, and prescribes self-knowledge (*ātmājñāna*) as the way to liberation.[14] Addressing and offering answers to basic questions about human existence, Advaita presents itself with a religious self-sufficiency and completeness that has little or no need for learning from other traditions and their practitioners.

The tradition, however, did not develop in isolation. Classical Advaita commentators, like Śaṅkara, engaged and disputed with both orthodox and nonorthodox traditions. In the process of doing so, Advaita absorbed elements of these traditions into its worldview, and the tradition was enriched. The purpose of traditional debates, however, was not mutual learning and enrichment but victory over one's opponent, which was celebrated in various traditional biographical narratives.[15] Today, in the teaching of Advaita, especially at traditional institutions of learning, the emphasis is on the classical interlocutors and on Śaṅkara's triumph in arguments with them. The concern is to affirm the superiority of Advaita over all other worldviews.

Although such debates are very interesting and historically enlightening, our context is now different, and Advaita in the twenty-first century has to engage new conversation partners with new motivations. The living traditions that ought to be our dialogue partners include Judaism, Christianity, Islam, and Buddhism as well as contemporary scientific and secular perspectives. The purpose of such conversations, however, has to be different from the classical times. The aim must be mutual enrichment through deep study and dialogue. In the course of such dialogue, we may find certain insights of another tradition to be attractive and compelling. When this happens, we must be prepared to incorporate and live out these truths. As Leonard Swidler reminded us decades ago, the readiness to change is a basic ground rule for dialogue: "We enter into dialogue so that we can learn, change, and grow, not so we can force change on the other, as one hopes to do in debate—a hope realized in inverse proportion to the frequency and ferocity with which debate is entered into."[16]

Given the historical self-sufficiency of Advaita representation, do we have a religious need for others? Could we enter into dialogue for mutual learning and enrichment? My answer to both questions is affirmative, even though these are not traditional Advaita positions. Acknowledging our theological need for others and being open to learning do not rule out engagement in positive and negative apologetics on behalf of a tradition and in its defense against rival views. In the words of Paul Griffiths, "If representative intellectuals belonging to some specific community come to judge at a particular time that some or all of their doctrine-expressing sentences are incompatible with some alien religious claim(s), then they should feel obliged to engage in both positive and negative apologetics vis-à-vis these alien religious claim(s) and their promulgators."[17] This is what

Śaṅkara and other Advaita commentators do, but they do so exclusively. There is no explicit acknowledgment of the value of other traditions, and the motivation, as noted already, is not learning but victory in argument.

More than any other Hindu tradition, Advaita, following the Upaniṣads, exemplifies a critical awareness of the limits of human language and other symbolic ways of communication in relation to the absolute One (*brahman*). No words can fully describe the intrinsic nature of *brahman*. The Taittirīya Upaniṣad (2.9.1) speaks of the absolute as that from which all words, with the mind, return having failed to reach. The Kena Upaniṣad (1.4) teaches that *brahman* is not the object of any word but the reality that makes all words known. In the language of paradox for which the Upaniṣads are famous, the Kena Upaniṣad (2.3) describes *brahman* as known to the one for whom it is unknown and unknown to the one for whom it is known. For those who know, it is not known; for those who do not know, it is known.

The limitation of language is also acknowledged in the Upaniṣads by the frequent use of apophatic language that speaks of *brahman* by telling us what it is not. Here are some examples:

> That which is invisible, ungraspable, without lineage, without color, without eyes or ears, without hands or feet, eternal, omnipresent, very subtle. That is the undiminishing, seen by the wise as the source of all. (Muṇḍaka Upaniṣad 1.1.6)

> One becomes freed from the jaws of death by knowing That which is wordless, untouched, formless, without taste, eternal, without scent, without beginning, without end, undecaying and greater than the great. (Kaṭha Upaniṣad 1.3.15)

> It is neither gross nor minute, neither short nor long,
> neither red color nor oiliness, neither shadow nor
> darkness, neither air nor ether, neither savor nor odor,
> without eyes or ears, without vocal organs or mind,
> nonluminous, without the vital force or mouth, not a
> measure, and without exterior or interior. It does not
> eat anything, nor is It eaten by anybody. (Bṛhadāraṇyaka
> Upaniṣad 1.4.7)

In his commentary on Bṛhadāraṇyaka Upaniṣad 1.4.7, Śaṅkara cautions us that even the most familiar and widely used words like *ātman* and *brahman* fall short. The absolute is beyond the scope of any term. In his commentary on the Bṛhadāraṇyaka Upaniṣad (2.1.20), Śaṅkara acknowledges that the words used in the scripture to speak about the absolute are finite human words from everyday usage. The scripture has no choice but to employ ordinary language to speak of the extraordinary.

Bhagavadgītā 2:29 speaks of the infinite *brahman* and repeats, three times, the Sanskrit word *āścaryavat*. *Āścaryavat* conveys a sense of wonder, marvel, and awe. *Brahman*, according to this Bhagavadgītā text, could be contemplated only with a sense of wonder (*āścaryavat paśyati kaścidenam*). One could speak of it only with wonder (*āścaryavadvadati tathaiva cānyaḥ*), and the one who hears does so with wonder (*āścaryavaccainam anyaḥ śṛṇoti*). This verse concludes with the observation that, even after hearing (*śrutvā api*), one never fully understands (*enam veda na caiva kaścit*).

This unmistakable recognition of finitude and the limits of human symbols in relation to *brahman* is an admonition against the absolutizing of any descriptions or definitions. We must resist the temptation of idolatry with words. Descriptions must be subjected, continuously, to critical inquiry that includes awareness of the social contexts in which these have been and are formulated. The implication is that we can only profess our traditions with humility and be open always to the possibility of learning from and being enriched by other traditions. This humility must extend across both inter- and intrareligious boundaries. Knowing the limits of our theology should open our hearts and minds to the richness of other theologies and their contributions to deepening our understanding. Religious diversity enriches our world theologically, and we are all diminished by its absence.

I have described in this work some of the ways in which dialogue with other traditions, especially Christianity, has enriched my Hindu self-understanding. The enrichment that I acknowledge is not only a deeper understanding of the nature of the divine but also further thinking about the divine-world relationship. Advaita (not-two) is an apophatic word that problematizes both "one" and "two" as descriptions of the divine-world relationship. Since it tells us, however, what the relationship is not, we are challenged to explore always what it means and to avoid glib formulas that falsely claim to be exhaustive statements.

My work as a Hindu scholar and committed member of my tradition continues to be enriched in other ways by my engagement with the Christian tradition and its practitioners and by methodologies developed for the study of sacred texts. This is especially true of my learning from Christian liberation theology. Traditional Hindu commentators and exegetes study these texts primarily as *mokṣa śāstra*—that is, as teachings meant for liberation. Many of the prominent interpreters, especially in the Advaita tradition, were renunciants who were ritually freed from both obligations of worship and the responsibilities of work in the world.[18] For the renunciant, there is little or no interest in the ways in which material, social, historical, or other factors influence the nature and content of a sacred text. Questions related to the historical formation of the text are not regarded as having any bearing on the central aim of attaining liberation or on the text as *mokṣa śāstra.*

The traditional reader who is a renouncer is also likely to belong to one of the upper castes, since eligibility to read was interpreted on the basis of the categories of caste and life-stage rights and duties (*varṇāśramadharma*). Within the confines of this socioreligious system, readership was limited to male members of the upper three castes. Women and members of the fourth caste (*śūdras*) were excluded, as well as the untouchables who were without caste. A male reader with an upper caste lineage is unlikely to problematize the hierarchy and injustices of caste or patriarchy. Śaṅkara, for example, though a renouncer and thus technically free from caste identity, is a defender of the traditional order and argues against the eligibility of *śūdras* to study the Vedas. "The *śūdra*," according to Śaṅkara, "has no competence, since he cannot study the Vedas; for one becomes competent for things spoken of in the Vedas, after one has studied the Vedas and known these things from them. But there can be no reading of the Vedas by a *śūdra*, for Vedic study presupposes the investiture with the sacred thread, which ceremony is confined to the three castes."[19]

Renunciant commentators with no interest in the social formation of a sacred text are similarly indifferent to the social implications of the text. Having severed family and social relationships, the implications of the texts for these are not matters to which he is likely to devote any exegetical energies. Such matters include the relevance of religious teachings for economies, law, and social and gender relationships. The significance of the text is narrowed by the exclusive lens of personal liberation.

Reading sacred texts through the lens of liberation theology does not exclude the traditional approach to the text as *mokṣa śāstra* but requires more. It requires attention to questions related to the historical formation of the text and questions related to the implications of the text for life in communities. Questions related to the historical formation of the text and its social context help us understand and question the hierarchies of exclusion and inclusion that are implicit in the text. Such factors may be invisible to the community within which the text is authoritative. A Hindu theologian who does not ask questions about the historical formation and social context of a sacred text is likely to treat the entire text as an ahistorical and authoritative source of teaching. Such a scholar has no rational grounds for questioning teachings and social structures that unjustly privilege certain groups and that exclude and marginalize others.

In addition to questions about the historical formation of the text and the material and the social and cultural factors that shape a tradition, reading the text through the lens of liberation theology also requires that we ask questions about the implications of the text for life in this world. What kinds of human relationships are commended, and which ones contradict the basic claims about the nature of human beings and ultimate reality? What are fundamental values, implicit or explicit in the text, that are normative for our lives in communities, families, and professions? What are our obligations to one another, to the planet, and to other species of life? Who in the text are the marginalized victims of injustice, and what are our responsibilities to them?

Admittedly, these are not the questions asked of the text by traditional commentators, and I was certainly not challenged to ask such questions when I studied at a traditional institution in India. In asking such questions, am I importing alien Christian and Western questions into the tradition? It would be dishonest not to acknowledge the influence of other traditions in the questions that I ask of the texts and the tradition and as sources for ideas such as structural injustice and institutionalized violence. My work is also informed by analysis drawn from the social sciences and from the methods of historical-critical study of religious traditions. Asking questions of one's tradition that are prompted by other traditions and employing methods of study developed elsewhere do not mean that one's theology lacks authenticity or is the product of another's influence. Such a conclusion denies my agency. I ask these new questions and employ these methods from a place of commitment to my tradition. It is as a Hindu and from a Hindu perspective that these questions interest me, and it is also from this place of commitment that I construct my theology. Learning from another tradition, like Christianity, is a process of deep discernment to ascertain the compatibility of theological insights and questions from another tradition with the core claims of one's own. Ultimately, my theology must find justification in these core claims and values and in interpretations that are faithful to the tradition's authoritative sources.

Deep encounters with another tradition have the potential to both challenge and enrich our traditions. I hope that the many ways in which my own work continues to benefit from such encounters serve as encouragement to other Hindu scholars to welcome the learning that dialogue affords. My theological need for people of other faiths is a realized fact, and I would not want to live in a world that is not beautifully and religiously diverse.

The divine impulse for creation in the Chāndogya Upaniṣad (6.2.3) is expressed in the wish to become many ("May I become many; may I grow forth"). There are lots of good reasons for understanding the "many" to include the many religious traditions of our world. These are fruits of divine self-expression that we must gratefully receive, celebrate, and learn from.

Notes

Foreword

1 See P. Podipara, *St. Thomas Christian Encyclopedia of India* (Trichur, India: STCEI, 1973), 2:107–12.

Introduction

1 Among these are Gregory Walter, Edmund Santurri, Torin Alexander, and Jamie Schillinger.
2 For summary reports of each of our meetings, see "Ethics in Action for Sustainable and Integral Development," End Slavery, accessed January 28, 2022, http://www.endslavery.va/content/endslavery/en/eia.html.
3 "Poems by Rabindranath Tagore," Poetry Foundation, accessed January 28, 2022, https://www.poetryfoundation.org/poetrymagazine/poems/55307/poems -56d236c1a2f9a.
4 All Bhagavadgītā citations are from the versions noted in the bibliography.
5 All Upaniṣad citations are from the versions noted in the bibliography.
6 All Chāndogya Upaniṣad quotations are from the versions noted in the bibliography.

Chapter One

1 See World Council of Churches, "Report from the Interreligious Consultation on 'Conversion—Assessing the Reality,'" *Current Dialogue*, no. 47 (June 2006), http://wcc-coe.org/wcc/what/interreligious/cd47-18.html.
2 "Christian Witness in a Multi-religious World: Recommendations for Conduct," Pontifical Council for Interreligious Dialogue, Vatican, accessed January 28, 2022, https://www.vatican.va/roman_curia/pontifical_councils/ interelg/documents/rc_pc_interelg_doc_20111110_testimonianza-cristiana_en .html. All quotations are taken from this version of the document. Hereafter abbreviated CWMW.
3 "The Orissa Freedom of Religion Act, 1967," Legislative Research (PRS), accessed January 28, 2022, https://www.indiacode.nic.in/bitstream/123456789/5957/1/ freedom_of_religion_act.pdf. All citations are taken from this source, 363–64.
4 *Bhagavadgita*, trans. Graham M. Schweig (New York: HarperSanFrancisco, 2007).

5 CWMW, principle 3.

6 CWMW, recommendation 1.

7 CWMW, principle 10.

8 See *Upaniṣads*, trans. Patrick Olivelle (New York: Oxford University Press, 2008).

9 "Eighth Assembly of the World Council of Churches: Harare, Zimbabwe, 3–14 December 1998," World Council of Churches, accessed February 2, 2022, http://www.wcc-coe.org/wcc/assembly/index-e.html.

10 *Padare* is a Shona word meaning meeting place. It speaks to a Zimbabwean tradition of people coming together to speak and learn from each other. See "*Padare* at the World Council of Churches Eighth Assembly," World Council of Churches, accessed January 28, 2022, http://www.wcc-coe.org/wcc/assembly/padare.html.

11 This presentation was given in one of the *padares* during the World Council of Churches Assembly in Harare, Zimbabwe, December 3–14, 1998. See "My God, Your God, Our God, No God," World Council of Churches, accessed January 28, 2022, http://wcc-coe.org/wcc/what/interreligious/cd33-13.html. I do not recollect the exact date at the assembly when I spoke.

12 Mahatma Gandhi, *All Men Are Brothers* (New York: Continuum, 1980), 1.

13 Maha Upaniṣad 6:71–72 in Sanskrit: *Ayaṃ nijaḥ paro veti gaṇanā laghucetasām udāracaritānāṃ tu vasudhaiva kuṭumbakam.*

14 S. Wesley Ariarajah, *The Bible and People of Other Faiths* (Geneva: World Council of Churches, 1985), 1.

15 Rowan Williams, *Tokens of Trust: An Introduction to Christian Belief* (Westminster: John Knox, 2010), 1.

16 Williams, 35.

17 *Śrī Rāmacaritamānasa*, trans. R. C. Prasad (Delhi: Motilal Banarsidass, 1984), 332.

18 *Śrī Rāmacaritamānasa*, Uttarakāṇḍa.

19 Douglas J. Schuurman, *Vocation: Discerning Our Callings in Life* (Grand Rapids, MI: Eerdmans, 2003), 7.

20 Quoted in Schuurman, 7.

21 This, of course, does not imply that all words are equal. Clearly, some word choices are better than others.

22 Quoted in Rachel Mikva, *Dangerous Religious Ideas: The Deep Roots of Self-Critical Faith in Judaism, Christianity, and Islam* (Boston: Beacon, 2020), 67.

23 Quoted in Mikva, 67.

24 CWMW, principle 3.

25 Hindu Vivek Kendra, *Religious Conversions* (Mumbai: Hindu Vivek Kendra, 1999), 15.

26 CWMW, principle 10.

27 M. K. Gandhi, *The Message of Jesus Christ*, ed. Anand T. Hingorani (Bombay: Bharatiya Vidya Bhavan, 1963), 36.

Chapter Two

1   "Statement from the Hindu-Christian Consultation Held in Varanasi, India, 23–26 October 1997," World Council of Churches, accessed January 28, 2022, http://wcc-coe.org/wcc/what/interreligious/cd31-05.html.

2   Klaus Klostermaier, "The Future of Hindu-Christian Dialogue," in *Hindu-Christian Dialogue*, ed. Harold Coward (Maryknoll, NY: Orbis, 1989), 265.

3   Harold Coward, "Hindu-Christian Dialogue: A Review," *Hindu-Christian Studies Bulletin* 1, no. 3 (Autumn 1988): 25–27.

4   Margaret Chatterjee, "The Prospect for Hindu-Christian Interaction," *Hindu-Christian Studies Bulletin* 2 (1989): 2.

5   See, for example, World Council of Churches, *Guidelines on Dialogue* (Geneva: World Council of Churches, 1979).

6   See chapter 1.

7   Ashok V. Chowgule, *Christianity in India: The Hindutva Perspective* (Mumbai: Hindu Vivek Kendra, 1999), 10.

8   S. Wesley Ariarajah, *Not without My Neighbour: Issues in Interfaith Relations* (Geneva: World Council of Churches, 1999), 74–75. I inserted the italicized word for clarification purposes.

9   V. D. Savarkar, *Hindutva* (New Delhi: Bharti Sahitya Sadan, 1989), 100–101.

10 For a good summary of Christian theologies of religion, see Paul Knitter, *Introducing Theologies of Religion* (Maryknoll, NY: Orbis, 2002).

11 Dayananda Saraswati, *Light of Truth*, trans. C. Bharadwaja (Delhi: Arya Pratinidhi Sabha, 1975), 648.

12 See R. D. Baird, "The Response of Swami Bhaktivedanta," in *Modern Responses to Religious Pluralism*, ed. Harold Coward (Albany: State University of New York Press, 1987), 123.

13 See Glyn Richards, *The Philosophy of Gandhi* (London: Curzon, 1982). For Sri Ramakrishna, see Ayon Maharaj, *Infinite Paths to Infinite Reality* (New York: Oxford University Press, 2018).

14 See Diana Eck, *Encountering God: A Spiritual Journey from Bozeman to Banaras* (Boston: Beacon, 1993). This is an insightful exploration of Hindu resources for thinking about religious diversity in relation to Christianity and other religions.

15 See Anantanand Rambachan, *Accomplishing the Accomplished: The Vedas as a Source of Valid Knowledge in Śaṅkara* (Honolulu: University of Hawaii Press, 1991).

16 Anantanand Rambachan, *The Limits of Scripture: A Critical Study of Vivekananda's Reinterpretation of the Authority of the Vedas* (Honolulu: University of Hawaii Press, 1994).

17 See, for example, Anantanand Rambachan, "The Nature and Authority of Scripture: Implications for Hindu-Christian Dialogue," *Hindu-Christian Studies Bulletin* 8, no. 4 (1995): 20–27.

18 See S. W. Ariarajah, "Pluralism and Harmony," *Current Dialogue* 25 (December 1993): 17–19.

19 Klostermaier, "Future of Hindu-Christian Dialogue," 265.

20 The work of Francis X. Clooney is a fine example of this tradition of careful exegesis in both traditions. See, for example, Francis X. Clooney, *Reading the Hindu and Christian Classics: Why and How Deep Learning Still Matters* (Charlottesville: University of Virginia Press, 2019).

21 Klostermaier, 266.

22 Francis X. Clooney, "The *Handbook* in Light of the Past and Future of Hindu-Christian Relations," in *The Routledge Handbook of Hindu-Christian Relations*, ed. Chad M. Bauman and Michelle Voss Roberts (Oxford: Routledge, 2021), 480.

23 Klostermaier, "Future of Hindu-Christian Dialogue," 264.

24 See Abraham Oommen and A. Pushparajan, *Issues in Hindu-Christian Relations* (Nagpur: National Council of Churches in India, 1996), 38.

25 See Anantanand Rambachan, "Are Religious Differences Only Semantic?," in *Words to Live By: Sacred Sources for Interreligious Engagement*, ed. Or N. Rose, Homayra Zaid, and Soren M. Hessler (Maryknoll, NY: Orbis, 2018), 17–18.

26 Some of our presentations were published in a special issue of the *Journal of Ecumenical Studies* 52, no. 1 (Winter 2017). Hans Ucko edited this volume. The essays here deal with the topics of pluralism, violence, and the other.

27 See Thomas Thangaraj, "Thinking Together: A Story and a Method," in *Religious Conversion: Religious Scholars Thinking Together*, ed. Shanta Premawardhana (West Sussex, UK: Wiley-Blackwell, 2015), 13. I am grateful to Thomas Thangaraj for so beautifully telling our story, and I draw in a special way from his account.

28 See Hans Ucko, ed., *Faces of the Other* (Geneva: World Council of Churches, 2005), 56–58.

29 Thangaraj, "Thinking Together," 14.

30 Eck, *Encountering God*, 223.

31 Eck, 222.

32 Shriman Narayan, *The Voice of Truth* (Ahmedabad: Navajivan Trust, 1969), 267.

33 Thangaraj, "Thinking Together," 19.

34 Eboo Patel, *Sacred Ground: Pluralism, Prejudice, and the Promise of America* (Boston: Beacon Press, 2012), 77–80.

Chapter Three

1 The organization is commonly referred to as the RSS. The RSS was founded in 1925 by a Maharashtrian brahmin named Keshavrao Baliram Hedgewar (1890–1940). Hedgewar was deeply influenced by the ideas of Savarkar and wanted to dedicate his life to the restoration of the unity of Hindu India. He was frustrated with Gandhi's nonviolent tactics and by the deep social, linguistic, and regional differences in India that he thought to be responsible for the conquest of India by the Muslims and the British. Hedgewar felt that the way forward was through a movement of inner transformation and the creation of an organization whose members were completely devoted to

the Indian nation. While the RSS has refused to become a political party in India, it has increasingly developed ties to parties and organizations that support its aims.

2 "Bharat Mata Ki Jai Should Be the Only Definition of Nationalism: Kher," *Hindustan Times*, accessed January 28, 2022, https://www.hindustantimes.com/india/bharat-mata-ki-jai-should-be-the-only-definition-of-nationalism-kher/story-yiuHuxHXTrcpOQUxGj94WJ.html.%7B~?~.

3 "Those Who Don't Say 'Bharat Mata Ki Jai' Have No Right to Stay in the Country: Fadnavis," *Times of India*, accessed January 28, 2022, https://timesofindia.indiatimes.com/india/Those-who-dont-say-Bharat-Mata-Ki-Jai-have-no-right-to-stay-in-country-Fadnavis/articleshow/51670103.cms.

4 "Say 'Bharat Mata Ki Jai' or You're Pakistani: MLA," *Tribune*, accessed January 28, 2022, https://www.tribuneindia.com/news/archive/nation/say-bharat-mata-ki-jai-or-you-re-pakistani-mla-550457.

5 For Christian possibilities, see "Is It Right for Christians to Say 'Bharat Mata Ki Jai'?," Marg, accessed January 28, 2022, https://margfamilies.com/christians-and-bharat-mata/?fbclid=IwAR1fnPqYL2m0ra0cjzBYE8MyVbgq5KwlEVy6W8Y0m1j6PWGyGUwJPdgfx-I.

6 See Chetan Bhatt, *Hindu Nationalism: Origins, Ideologies and Modern Myths* (Oxford: Berg, 2001).

7 Savarkar, *Hindutva*, 82. All references are from this edition.

8 Savarkar, 88–90. The term *jāti* is commonly used today to designate a caste group.

9 Savarkar, 91.

10 Savarkar, 101.

11 Savarkar, 113.

12 See *Upaniṣads*, trans. Patrick Olivelle (New York: Oxford University Press, 2008).

13 Swami Vivekananda, *The Complete Works of Swami Vivekananda*, ed. Mayavati Memorial, 8 vols. (Kolkata: Advaita Ashrama, 1964–71). Hereafter cited as *CW*. The volume number is indicated after the letters *CW*, with pages given after the colon. See *CW* 1:6–20.

14 *CW* 3:366–84.

15 *CW* 3:105.

16 Ainslie T. Embree, "Vivekananda and Indian Nationalism," in *Swami Vivekananda Centenary Memorial Volume*, ed. R. C. Majumdar (Calcutta: Swami Vivekananda Centenary, 1963), 519–24.

17 *Bhagavadgītā*, trans. Winthrop Sargeant (Albany: State University of New York Press, 1984).

18 My translation.

19 Mahatma Gandhi, *All Men Are Brothers* (New York: Columbia University Press, 1958), 89.

20 This does not deny the reality of exclusivism in Hinduism. The point is that the predominant orientation of the tradition is pluralistic in its approach to its own internal diversity and, by extension, to other faiths.

21 M. S. Golwalkar Guruji, *We or Our Nationhood Defined* (Nagpur, India: Bharat, 1939), http://www.culturism.us/booksummaries/We%20or%20our%20 Nationhood%20Defined%20Newer%20PDF.pdf.

22 See Khyati Joshi, *White Christian Privilege: The Illusion of Religious Equality in America* (New York: New York University Press, 2020).

Chapter Four

1 "Key Findings about the Religious Composition of India," Pew Research Center, accessed January 29, 2022, https://www.pewresearch.org/fact-tank/ 2021/09/21/key-findings-about-the-religious-composition-of-india/.

2 "Why India Needs More Reliable Data on Dalit Christians and Muslims," Scroll .in, accessed January 29, 2022, https://scroll.in/article/989608/why-india-needs -more-reliable-data-on-dalit-christians-and-muslims.

3 "Why Are Many Indian Muslims Seen as Untouchable," BBC News, accessed January 29, 2022, https://www.bbc.com/news/world-asia-india-36220329.

4 See Gail Omvedt, *Buddhism in India: Challenging Brahmanism and Caste*, 3rd ed. (New Delhi: Sage, 2014).

5 "Dr. Ambedkar's Politics and Spirituality," Asian Voice, accessed January 29, 2022, https://www.asian-voice.com/Opinion/Columnists/Hari-Desai/Dr. -Ambedkar%E2%80%99s-Politics-and-Spirituality.

6 B. R. Ambedkar, "Away from the Hindus," in *Essays on Untouchables and Untouchability*, accessed January 29, 2022, http://www.ambedkar.org/ambcd/ 25.%20Essay%20on%20Untouchables%20and%20Untouchability_Religious .htm#c01.

7 Ambedkar.

8 See Prabhati Mukherjee, *Beyond the Four Varnas: The Untouchables in India* (Shimla: Indian Institute of Advanced Study, 1988), 18–19.

9 See Mukherjee, chap. 2.

10 "SCs, STs Form 25% of the Population, Says Census 2011 Data," *Indian Express*, accessed January 29, 2022, http://archive.indianexpress.com/news/scs-sts-form -25--of-population-says-census-2011-data/1109988/.

11 See Isabel Wilkerson, *Caste: The Origins of Our Discontents* (New York: Random House, 2020), 17.

12 D. S. Sarma, *Essence of Hinduism* (Mumbai: Bharatiya Vidya Bhavan, 1971), 54.

13 Vivekanand Jha, "Caste, Untouchability and Social Justice: Early North Indian Perspective," *Social Scientist* 25, nos. 11/12 (November–December 1997): 19–30.

14 Ruhi Tewari and Abhishek Mishra, "Every Second ST, Every Third Dalit & Muslim in India Poor, Not Just Financially: UN Report," ThePrint, July 12, 2019, https://theprint.in/india/every-second-st-every-third-dalit-muslim-in -india-poor-not-just-financially-un-report/262270/.

15 Sonalde Desai and Amaresh Dubey, "Caste in 21st Century India: Competing Narratives," *Economic and Political Weekly* 46, no. 11 (March 2012): 40–49,

https://www.ncbi.nlm.nih.gov/pmc/articles/PMC3379882/. See also Ajit Kumar Jha, "The Dalits: Still Untouchable," *India Today*, February 15, 2016, https://www.indiatoday.in/magazine/the-big-story/story/20160215-dalits -untouchable-rohith-vemula-caste-discrimination-828418-2016-02-03.

16 Chowgule, *Christianity in India*, 49–50.

17 See Swami Dayananda Saraswati, "Conversion Is an Act of Violence," SwamiJ.com, accessed January 29, 2022, https://www.swamij.com/conversion-violence.htm.

18 Sathianathan Clarke, "The Promise of Religious Conversion: Exploring Approaches, Exposing Myths, Exploring Modalities," in *Crossing Religious Borders: Studies on Conversion and Religious Belonging*, ed. Christine Lienemann-Perrin and Wolfgang Lienemann (Weisbaden: Harrossowitz Verlag, 2012), 602.

19 Thomas Thangaraj, "The Missiological Hermeneutics of a Convert," *Exchange* 32, no. 1 (2015): 3–41.

20 Clarke, "Promise of Religious Conversion," 605.

21 Kancha Ilaiah, *Why I Am Not a Hindu* (Delhi: Samya, 1996), 1.

22 Ilaiah, 1.

23 Joe Jose, "Caste in Christianity," *Dalit Camera* 3 (July 2020), https://www .dalitcamera.com/caste-in-christianity-2/.

24 Swaminathan Natarajan, "Indian Dalits Find No Refuge from Caste in Christianity," BBC Tamil, September 14, 2010, https://www.bbc.com/news/ world-south-asia-11229170.

25 T. A. Ameerudheen, "Is the Caste System Deep-Rooted among Christians in India? A Kerala Bishop Stirs Up a Hornet's Nest," Scroll.in, April 20, 2018, https://scroll.in/article/876000/is-the-caste-system-deep-rooted-among -christians-in-india-a-kerala-bishop-stirs-up-a-hornets-nest.

26 B. R. Ambedkar, *Annihilation of Caste*, ed. and annot. S. Anand, with an introduction by Arundhati Roy (London: Verso, 2014), 282.

27 From the Hindu perspective, I have explored such resources in Anantanand Rambachan, *A Hindu Theology of Liberation: Not-Two Is Not One* (Albany: State University of New York Press, 2015), chap. 9.

28 See Sadhana Coalition of Progressive Hindus, "A Hindu Apology for Caste and Untouchability," Action Network, accessed January 29, 2022, https:// actionnetwork.org/forms/a-hindu-apology-for-caste-and-untouchability. See also Anantanand Rambachan, "Hindu Temples Must Be Open to All," anantanand.com, April 4, 2016, https://anantrambachan.com/articles/hindu -temples-must-be-open-to-all.

Chapter Five

1 The chapter is a revised version of the "Brien O'Brien and Mary Hasten Lecture in Interreligious Dialogue," that I delivered at Boston College, MA, on November 7, 2019. I am grateful to Professor Catherine Cornille for inviting me to deliver this special lecture.

2 See Stanley Samartha, *The Hindu Response to the Unbound Christ* (Bangalore: Christian Institute for the Study of Religion and Society, 1974), 26.

3 Keshub Chunder Sen, *The Brahmo Samaj: Four Lectures* (London: W. H. Allen, 1870), 26.

4 Sen, 29–30.

5 Sri Ramakrishna and Swami Vivekananda, "The Baranagore Math," accessed January 29, 2022, https://www.ramakrishnavivekananda.info/swamieastwest/2_files/1-12.html.

6 M. M. Thomas, *The Acknowledged Christ of the Indian Renaissance* (Madras: Christian Literature Society, 1970), 205.

7 Rajmohan Gandhi, *Why Gandhi Still Matters* (New Delhi: Aleph, 2017), 59–60.

8 *CW* 8:328.

9 Martin Luther King Jr., *Stride toward Freedom: The Montgomery Story* (New York: Harper, 1958), 97.

10 See World Council of Churches, *Religious Resources for a Just Society: A Hindu-Christian Dialogue* (Geneva: World Council of Churches, 1981).

11 "Matthew 24; Matthew 25," Bible Study Tools, accessed January 29, 2022, https://www.biblestudytools.com/matthew/passage/?q=matthew+24;+matthew+25.

12 See Rambachan, *Hindu Theology of Liberation*.

13 For a good short discussion, see Diana Eck, *Darśan: Seeing the Divine Image in India* (New York: Columbia University Press, 1998).

14 See *CW* 1:328.

15 Gandhi, *Message of Jesus Christ*, 23.

Chapter Six

1 This chapter is a revised version of a lecture that I delivered at Valparaiso University (Valparaiso, IN, October 3, 2019) as the 2019 John Martin Gross and Clara Amanda Gross Memorial Lecturer. I am grateful to Professor George Pati for inviting me.

2 See Anantanand Rambachan, "A Hindu Looks at Jesus," *Theology* 88, no. 774 (July 1985): 255–59.

3 See *Upaniṣads*, trans. P. Olivelle (Oxford: Oxford University Press, 1996); also *Upaniṣads*, trans. and ed. V. J. Roebuck (London: Penguin, 2003). Translations modified.

4 Williams, *Tokens of Trust*, 11.

5 Bṛhadāraṇyaka Upaniṣad 5.1.1 in Sanskrit: *Om pūrṇamadaḥ pūrṇamidaṁ pūrṇāt pūrṇamudacayate.*

    Pūrṇasya pūrṇamādāya pūrṇamevāvaśiṣyate.

6 Eck, *Encountering God*, 140–41.

7 "Psalms 139:1–24," Bible.com, accessed January 29, 2022, https://www.bible.com/bible/114/PSA.139.1-24.NKJV.

8 See Marcus Borg, *The God We Never Knew* (New York: HarperCollins, 1997). I have discussed some of Borg's views in relation to Advaita in Anantanand Rambachan, "Advaita Vedanta and Marcus Borg: Opportunities for Hindu-Christian Dialogue," *Hindu-Christian Studies Bulletin* 16, no. 8 (2003): 30–37.

9 Borg, *God We Never Knew*, 65–68.

10 Borg, 77.

Chapter Seven

1 See Conrad Hackett and David McClendon, "Christians Remain the World's Largest Religious Group, but They Are Declining in Europe," Pew Research Center, April 5, 2017, https://www.pewresearch.org/fact-tank/2017/04/05/christians-remain-worlds-largest-religious-group-but-they-are-declining-in-europe/.

2 Diana Eck, *A New Religious America: How a "Christian Country" Has Become the World's Most Religiously Diverse Nation* (San Francisco: HarperSanFrancisco, 2002).

3 W. C. Smith, *The Faith of Other Men* (New York: Harper and Row, 1963), 11.

4 See World Council of Churches, *Religious Resources*.

5 Paul Knitter, "Interreligious Dialogue: What? Why? How?," in *Interreligious Dialogue: An Anthology of Voices Bridging Cultural and Religious Divides*, ed. Christoffer H. Grundmann (Winona, MN: Anselm Academic, 2015), 37.

6 *CW* 3:40.

7 Mahatma Gandhi, *All Men Are Brothers*, 68.

8 Gandhi, 81.

9 For more substantial arguments, see Rambachan, *Hindu Theology of Liberation*.

10 *CW* 3:40.

11 Ariarajah, *Not without My Neighbour*, 14.

12 See Anantanand Rambachan, "Interreligious Dialogue: The Political and Theological," HuffPost, last updated June 21, 2015, https://www.huffpost.com/entry/interreligious-dialogue-the-political-and-theological_b_7103124.

13 For an exploration of the meaning of not-two, see Anantanand Rambachan, "Rethinking the One and the Many in Advaita," in *The Routledge Handbook of Hindu-Christian Relations*, ed. Chad M. Bauman and Michelle Voss Roberts (London: Routledge, 2021), 355–68.

14 For a detailed discussion of the Advaita tradition, see Anantanand Rambachan, *The Advaita Worldview: God, World and Humanity* (Albany: State University of New York Press, 2006).

15 "The Biography of Adi Shankaracharya," sringeri.net, accessed January 29, 2022, https://sringeri.net/history/sri-adi-shankaracharya/biography/abridged-madhaviya-shankara-digvijayam#vedic-india-in-the-8th-century-ad.

16 Leonard Swidler, "The Dialogue Decalogue," Grand Valley State University, accessed January 19, 2022, https://www.gvsu.edu/cms4/asset/843249C9-B1E5-BD47-A25EDBC68363B726/dialoguedecalogue.pdf.

17 See Paul J. Griffiths, *An Apology for Apologetics: A Study in the Logic of Interreligious Dialogue* (Eugene, OR: Wipf & Stock, 2007), 3.

18 See Patrick Olivelle, *Saṃnyasa Upanishads: Hindu Scriptures on Asceticism and Renunciation* (New York: Oxford University Press, 2006).

19 Swami Gambhirananda, trans., *Brahmasutra Bhasya of Sankaracarya* (Calcutta: Advaita Ashrama, 1986), 1.3.38.

Bibliography

Primary Sources in English Translation

The Bhagavadgītā. Translated by Swami Dayananda Saraswati. Chennai: Arsha Vidya Centre, 2007.

The Bhagavadgītā. Translated by Winthrop Sargeant. Albany: State University of New York Press, 1984.

The Bhagavadgita. Translated by Graham M. Schweig. New York: HarperSanFrancisco, 2007.

The Bhagavadgītā with the Commentary of *Śaṅkarācārya*. Translated by Alladi Mahadeva Sastry. Madras: Samata Books, 1977.

Brahmasūtra Bhaṣya of Śaṅkarācārya. Translated by Swami Gambhirananda. Calcutta: Advaita Ashrama, 1977.

Bṛhadāraṇyaka Upaniṣad with the Commentary of Śaṅkarācārya. Translated by Swami Madhavananda. Calcutta: Advaita Ashrama, 1975.

Chāndogya Upaniṣad. Translated by Swami Swahananda. Madras: Sri Ramakrishna Math, 1975.

Chāndogya Upaniṣad with the Commentary of Śaṅkara. Translated by Ganganatha Jha. Poona: Oriental Book Agency, 1942.

Eight Upaniṣads with the Commentary of Śaṅkarācārya. Translated by Swami Gambhirananda. 2 vols. Īśa, Kena, Kaṭha, and Taittirīya in vol. 1; Aitaraya, Muṇḍaka, Māṇḍūkya and Kārika, and Praśna in vol. 2. Calcutta: Advaita Ashrama, 1965–1966.

Ramayana of Valmiki. Translated by Hari Prasad Shastri. 3 vols. London: Shanti Sadan, 1957–1962.

Śrī Rāmacaritamānasa. Translated by R. C. Prasad. Delhi: Motilal Banarsidass, 1984.

Śvetāśvatara Upaniṣad. Translated by Swami Gambhirananda. Calcutta: Advaita Ashrama, 1986.

The Upanishads. Translated by Patrick Olivelle. Oxford: Oxford University Press, 1996.

The Upaniṣads. Translated and edited by Valerie J. Roebuck. London: Penguin, 2003.

Secondary Sources

Ambedkar, B. R. *Annihilation of Caste*. Edited and annotated by S. Anand. London: Verso, 2014.

Ariarajah, Wesley S. *The Bible and People of Other Faiths*. Geneva: World Council of Churches, 1985.

———. *Not without My Neighbour: Issues in Interfaith Relations*. Geneva: World Council of Churches, 1999.

Bauman, Chad M., and Michelle Voss Roberts, eds. *The Routledge Handbook of Hindu-Christian Relations*. Oxford: Routledge, 2021.

Bhatt, Chetan. *Hindu Nationalism: Origins, Ideologies and Modern Myths*. Oxford: Berg, 2001.

Borg, Marcus. *The God We Never Knew*. New York: HarperCollins, 1997.

Chowgule, Ashok. *Christianity in India: The Hindutva Perspective*. Mumbai: Hindu Vivek Kendra, 1999.

Clooney, Francis X. *Reading the Hindu and Christian Classics: Why and How Deep Learning Still Matters*. Charlottesville: University of Virginia Press, 2019.

Coward, Harold, ed. *Hindu-Christian Dialogue*. Maryknoll, NY: Orbis, 1989.

———, ed. *Modern Responses to Religious Pluralism*. Albany: State University of New York Press, 1987.

Eck, Diana L. *Darśan: Seeing the Divine Image in India*. New York: Columbia University Press, 1998.

———. *Encountering God: A Spiritual Journey from Bozeman to Banaras*. Boston: Beacon, 1993.

———. *A New Religious America: How a "Christian Country" Has Become the World's Most Religiously Diverse Nation*. San Francisco: HarperSanFrancisco, 2002.

Gandhi, Mahatma. *All Men Are Brothers*. New York: Continuum, 1980.

———. *The Message of Jesus Christ*. Edited by Anand T. Hingorani. Bombay: Bharatiya Vidya Bhavan, 1963.

Gandhi, Rajmohan. *Why Gandhi Still Matters*. New Delhi: Aleph Books, 2017.

Griffiths, Paul J. *An Apology for Apologetics: A Study in the Logic of Interreligious Dialogue*. Eugene, OR: Wipf & Stock, 2007.

Grundmann, Christoffer H., ed. *Interreligious Dialogue: An Anthology of Voices Bridging Cultural and Religious Divides*. Winona, MN: Anselm Academic, 2015.

Hindu Vivek Kendra. *Religious Conversions*. Mumbai: Hindu Vivek Kendra, 1999.

Ilaiah, Kancha. *Why I Am Not a Hindu*. Delhi: Samya, 1996.

Joshi, Khyati. *White Christian Privilege: The Illusion of Religious Equality in America*. New York: New York University Press, 2020.

King, Martin Luther, Jr. *Stride toward Freedom: The Montgomery Story*. New York: Harper, 1958.

Knitter, Paul. *Introducing Theologies of Religion*. Maryknoll, NY: Orbis, 2002.

Lienemann-Perrin, Christine, and Wolfgang Lienemann, eds. *Crossing Religious Borders: Studies on Conversion and Religious Belonging*. Weisbaden: Harrossowitz Verlag, 2012.

Maharaj, Ayon. *Infinite Paths to Infinite Reality*. New York: Oxford University Press, 2018.

Meghwanshi, Bhanwar. *I Could Not Be Hindu*. New Delhi: Navyana, 2020.

Mikva, Rachel. *Dangerous Religious Ideas: The Deep Roots of Self-Critical Faith in Judaism, Christianity, and Islam*. Boston: Beacon, 2020.

Mukherjee, Prabhati. *Beyond the Four Varnas: The Untouchables in India*. Shimla: Indian Institute of Advanced Study, 1988.

Olivelle, Patrick. *Saṃnyasa Upanishads: Hindu Scriptures on Asceticism and Renunciation*. New York: Oxford University Press, 2006.

Omvedt, Gail. *Buddhism in India: Challenging Brahmanism and Caste*. 3rd ed. New Delhi: Sage, 2014.

Oommen, Abraham, and A. Pushparajan. *Issues in Hindu-Christian Relations*. Nagpur: National Council of Churches in India, 1996.

Patel, Eboo. *Sacred Ground: Pluralism, Prejudice and the Promise of America*. Boston: Beacon, 2012.

Premawardhana, Shanta, ed. *Religious Conversion: Religious Scholars Thinking Together*. West Sussex, UK: Wiley-Blackwell, 2015.

Rambachan, Anantanand. *Accomplishing the Accomplished: The Vedas as a Source of Valid Knowledge in Śaṅkara*. Honolulu: University of Hawaii Press, 1991.

———. "Advaita Vedanta and Marcus Borg: Opportunities for Hindu-Christian Dialogue." *Hindu-Christian Studies Bulletin* 16, no. 8 (2003): 30–37.

———. *The Advaita Worldview: God, World and Humanity*. Albany: State University of New York Press, 2006.

———. "A Hindu Looks at Jesus." *Theology* 88, no. 774 (July 1985): 255–259.

———. *A Hindu Theology of Liberation: Not-Two Is Not One*. Albany: State University of New York Press, 2015.

———. *The Limits of Scripture: A Critical Study of Vivekananda's Reinterpretation of the Authority of the Vedas*. Honolulu: University of Hawaii Press, 1994.

Richards, Glyn. *The Philosophy of Gandhi*. London: Curzon, 1982.

Samartha, Stanley. *The Hindu Response to the Unbound Christ*. Bangalore: Christian Institute for the Study of Religion and Society, 1974.

Saraswati, Dayananda. *Light of Truth*. Translated by C. Bharadwaja. Delhi: Arya Pratinidhi Sabha, 1975.

Sarma, D. S. *Essence of Hinduism*. Mumbai: Bharatiya Vidya Bhavan, 1971.

Savarkar, V. D. *Hindutva*. New Delhi: Bharti Sahitya Sadan, 1989.

Schuurman, Douglas J. *Vocation: Discerning Our Callings in Life*. Grand Rapids, MI: Eerdmans, 2003.

Sen, Keshub Chunder. *The Brahmo Samaj: Four Lectures*. London: W. H. Allen, 1870.

Thomas, M. M. *The Acknowledged Christ of the Indian Renaissance*. Madras: Christian Literature Society, 1970.

Ucko, Hans, ed. *Faces of the Other*. Geneva: World Council of Churches, 2005.

Vivekananda, Swami. *The Complete Works of Swami Vivekananda*. 8 vols. Mayavati Memorial ed. Kolkata: Advaita Ashrama, 1964–1971.

Wilkerson, Isabel. *Caste: The Origins of Our Discontents*. New York: Random House, 2020.

Williams, Rowan. *Tokens of Trust: An Introduction to Christian Belief.* Louisville, KY: Westminster John Knox, 2010.

World Council of Churches. *Religious Resources for a Just Society: A Hindu-Christian Dialogue.* Geneva: World Council of Churches, 1981.

Yengde, Suraj. *Caste Matters.* Gurgaon: Penguin Viking India, 2019.

Index